The

PTSD WIVES HANDBOOK

Her Guide to Inner Peace, Self-Love,
and Personal Strength

Write It Out
PUBLISHING, LLC

VIRGINIA BEACH, VA

Printed by Kiyanni B., Write It Out Publishing, LLC. in the United States of America.

Write It Out Publishing LLC
Virginia Beach, Virginia
Writeitoutpublishing.com

ISBN: 979-8-9869842-9-2

Book Cover Illustrator:

Editor: Tamira K. Butler-Likely & Renee Johnson

First printing, e-book & paperback, December 2022
Author: Coach Leah N. Huggins
Ocean Springs, MS 39564
info@iamcoachleah.com
www.iamcoachleah.com
www.marriagemotherhoodptsd.com

The

PTSD WIVES HANDBOOK

Her Guide to Inner Peace, Self-Love,
and Personal Strength

By
Coach Leah N. Huggins

Contents

Dedication

To My Husband:

For every tear, every heartache, and every storm in our life there has been an abundance of love, respect, and adoration. For better or worse, in sickness and in health, we've done it all. But we did it together. The storms couldn't break us, and 21 years later, I still say yes.

Foreword
Pattern Pathway Power

This is an essential handbook with information, explanation, and steps to empower wives to be their best while supporting a spouse who has survived trauma on any level of life. It unfolds "Pattern, Pathway, and Power," which are essential ingredients of this handbook. It will challenge, change, and make you a champion wife and a better you.

Leah has made the decision to be transparent, which is the best way to help wives so they can realize, "I am not the only one and someone else understands what I'm going through." She has taken her struggles and setbacks and turned them into steps of success. Every reader endeavoring to support a spouse with PTSD will be able to take the steps she has given and start a new beginning for a successful tomorrow.

Her words are authentic and a necessary pattern that can give one the power to bring change. Regardless of the level of your life, everyone needs a pattern. By reading this handbook you will learn ways to cut down the jungles of life in order to clear your path to joyful success.

Leah faced herself first and then cut a new pathway through the jungle of her circumstances. She unfolds the process needed for you to produce a new level of progress. Using this handbook will enlighten, exercise, and give you the motivation needed to move in a positive direction. You will be able to measure moments and take steps into your new pathway.

As you read, listen to the words of sincerity, because she has lived through it. It's not hype, clichés, or someone else's words. She decided to confront, challenge, and make her personal change that resulted in the power to apply and overcome. Her words are weighted.

I've seen, heard, and watched her persevere. Her tears were a sign that expressed "I must, I can, and I will live through this." Her mental determination gave her spirit inspiration. She understood "my fight is bigger than me. This is for my sanity and for my family."

So, let this handbook bless you. Make it a keeper. Then think of someone else who may need these words to help them create a new pattern and clear a pathway to bring power to their life. This book will give the fuel needed to make change and produce a champion.

Sincerely,
Dr. Vance L. Woods
A.A., B.Th., MTh, D. Min.

Introduction

Dear PTSD Wife,

I can remember seeking help from a "professional" about the things I was going through with my husband concerning his PTSD. I left feeling like it was all my fault for "enabling" him to continue behaving in this way.

Yes...the EASY solution would be not to take his crap anymore and just leave. But not if you want your marriage to work.

If you leave, the monster (PTSD) wins.

Don't get me wrong...I DON'T BELIEVE ANYONE SHOULD STAY IN A TOXIC, ABUSIVE RELATIONSHIP. Your health and safety (and that of your family) should be your #1 priority. I am referring to being unhappy in your relationship because of the circumstances surrounding your problems.

MARRIAGE CAN SURVIVE PTSD!! But as with anything, you must have the proper tools to be successful.

WHAT I LEARNED:

You can't always change the situation...but you can change yourself to better deal with your situation.

WHAT DOES THAT MEAN?

By changing yourself—changing the way you think, the way you process your emotions, and the way you react in adversity—you can change your situation.

I am on a mission to help women to Reclaim Their Power so they can Take Back Their Life! Together we can do this.

COACH LEAH

Chapter 1: I Am Not Okay

I know what it's like to be broken. To be empty inside. So many sleepless nights, whispering through tears, "I just want to be happy."

The truth is, PTSD affects the whole house, not just the person that has experienced the trauma. As the spouse of someone that is working to manage their symptoms, you must be careful to protect your own emotional wellbeing. You are responsible for your own happiness. It's your life. You are in control of your own destiny. What you choose to accept is your own decision. Know your limits and what you are able to handle, and what you are willing and not willing to accept.

You've got a decision to make. Ask yourself:

1. What is it that you sincerely want from your relationship at this moment?

2. Can you live with your decision if you choose to stay? If you choose to leave?

3. Can you deal with being alone? Can you continue living like you are now?

4. How much can you handle?

These are questions that I was asked when I was in the same predicament. Here's my story.

My husband and I are both proud Navy Veterans. He served two tours in Iraq during the war, after which he was diagnosed with PTSD, depression, and anxiety. Our relationship suffered and we struggled to maintain our marriage.

I would be doing a disservice to you by having you believe that all the problems in my marriage were due to my husband's conditions. PTSD did not cause the problems in my marriage. Most of the problems were already there. What PTSD did was highlight those issues. I came into the marriage with my own set of issues and problems, and he did too. That, coupled together with the effect that PTSD has on a relationship, created a hostile environment in our home.

For years, I wore a mask, a forced smile and cheerful disposition, pretending that everything was okay on the outside. But on the inside, I was slowly dying; crumbling away as the toxic environment surrounding me chipped away at my soul bit by bit. I dealt with anxiety, depression, fear, and doubt; living in a constant state of inner turmoil. Little by little, I released control over certain areas of my life. I let anxiety take my peace, depression take my joy, and fear take my sanity. I allowed doubt to rob me of my confidence and self-esteem. Insecurity and shame stripped me of meaningful relationships. As loneliness set in, isolation, depression, and hopelessness were right behind.

It seemed my world had spiraled out of control. My marriage suffered as I had become emotionally disconnected and fell into a deep depression of my own. It seemed everyone was against me. There were days I could not get out of bed. I was angry and upset with everyone. Because of that, my relationships suffered at home, at work, and even at church. I was in a dark place. The goal of a PTSD Wife is to be supportive and understanding. But it's hard to extend that same love and grace to someone else when you haven't yet extended it to yourself.

Where your mind goes, your body will follow. Emotional distress will eventually begin to manifest in the physical and can cause serious health problems. After a while, my body began to react to the stress it was under, and I began to suffer with unnecessary health issues. Migraines, tension headaches, high blood pressure, and even excessive weight gain all told the story. I was not taking care of myself.

At some point it seemed as if there was no escape from the situation, even if I wanted to. I had become totally financially dependent and unable to be self-sufficient. My life and wellbeing depended on factors that were outside of my control. Looking back now, I can see where I had given up. I felt defeated and let go of hope. This was my life for years before I finally decided that enough was enough.

There was no one moment that sparked the change; no one thing that I can attribute to the turnaround that happened in my life. Instead, it was a series of small steps that eventually put me on the right path. It didn't happen overnight. It didn't even happen on purpose. It was a process, and as I began to do the work, I noticed the changes that were happening within and around me.

I gained control of my life once I decided that I no longer wanted to be a product of my environment. I wanted off the emotional rollercoaster. I needed stability and I was no longer willing to let life just happen to me. I had to come to the realization that my happiness is my responsibility and no one else's. I had to learn how to keep my joy regardless of the circumstance and not be swayed by the words and actions of others.

I changed my environment by first changing the way that I think, learning that self-care was not selfish, but in fact a necessity. I began to take better care of myself, mind, body, and soul, and let go of emotional baggage through the process of forgiveness and began to heal from the inside out. Eventually, I did reclaim my power and was able to take back my life.

I decided to stay in my marriage because I knew what we once were, and I believed I could get back to that and make it even better. Don't get me wrong, it wasn't easy. There were days that we both wanted to quit. The turning point for us was when we decided to take the "D Word" off the table. We would no longer threaten divorce to get our own way anymore. We wanted to fight for our marriage, and FIGHT is what we had to do. We had to pull ourselves out of the hole we had dug together. It wasn't easy.

There were some days that it felt like I was doing all the work, and some days he felt he was doing all the work. We learned that the process of fixing a marriage relies mainly on fixing YOURSELF for your marriage. I had to ask myself, "What is MY role in fixing my marriage?" That is when I realized the assignment is not to change him, but to change ME! I decided to stop waiting on someone else to make me happy. My happiness was up to me and not reliant on the actions of others.

He is not the problem. The real problem is the spirit behind the actions that a person takes. I had to shift my focus and learn how to deal with the spirit and not attack HIM as the problem. Once I fix ME, everything else will fall in line. Working on me helped me to change my focus. I changed the way I saw him by changing the way I thought about him. I took responsibility for my own actions and stopped blaming him, or others, for what I was not able to control.

People stay in toxic relationships because they fear the unknown and end up getting comfortable sitting in dysfunction. They don't want to go through anything that takes them out of their comfort zone that will take work and will require more effort from them. It's easy to quit, or to give up, but they will end up missing the opportunity to grow and learn and most importantly, to see how God can bring you out of your mess and work a miracle on your behalf. Yes, sticking it out is the road less traveled.

If you have a choice to make, know that God is with you no matter your decision. That was the piece of advice I needed to give me solace and the strength I needed to stay in the fight for my marriage. You are a product of your decisions. Have faith in yourself and have faith in God to bring you through. You won't be disappointed.

Much like the healing process, my journey to becoming a support for other PTSD Wives came over time and began with small steps. I like to call them God-nudges. It was more of an awareness of how common the struggles were among women who have spouses that have experienced trauma.

Life is going to have its ups and downs, but real peace comes from within. It is not based on what is going on outside of a person. It requires changing the way you think about your situation. Your mindset is key in making life changes. Whatever you want to do, it must first start with a thought. What you visualize will become your goal. When you have a goal, you can create a plan. When you put an action behind that plan, you will create the change you desire.

By reading this book and putting the principles into action, you will be well on your path to inner peace, self-love, confidence, and personal strength. You will turn your fear into fuel, and pain into purpose. You will finally grab hold of the power that already lies within, and you will be able to take back the control of your life. You will discover and renew your passion and turn it into purpose, which will eventually turn into profit. Through the transformation of your mind, you will become the master of your destiny and create the life you desire. The Key to Success: COMMIT TO THE PROCESS.

There is power in community, and you are not alone. I wrote this book to let you know that you no longer have to suffer in silence. It's time to get off the emotional rollercoaster and stand firm in your power. Not just for yourself, but for the people that are connected to you and your purpose. The world needs you to be who you were created to be.

So where do you start? RIGHT HERE! We've already begun. Your journey started when you took the first step and picked up this book. Congratulations on making this most important decision for change. I am here to cheer you on and guide you along the way.

Now, let's get moving! I'll meet you on the other side.

Chapter 2: Through the Storm

I live in the South. Every year, we prepare for a new storm season. It is in the hot summer months that the tropics are most active. Now, some rain is good. We need it because it is the rain that makes things grow. It creates a healthy natural environment that gives life and adds color and beauty to the world around us.

But every now and then, there comes a storm that changes everything. This storm is dangerous. It uproots at the foundation and turns to chaos to everything in its path. The damage is irreparable. Unfortunately, many people don't survive this type of storm.

I look at the damage done by Hurricane Katrina in 2005, and I remember how beautiful and full of life the Gulf Coast was before the storm. For safety, I evacuated and headed north to be with family, well out of the danger zone. Once the storm cleared, I headed home. The effects of the storm were so far reaching. Hours away from where the storm hit, you could see how the trees that once lined the highways were all leaning back, almost laying down. A testament to the power and force of the winds of that storm. The closer I got, the more damage I saw. Houses were swept away from their foundations; traffic lights and power lines were down. Flood waters trapped cars and carried them away. Debris was everywhere and it was impossible to tell one neighborhood from another because of so much devastation and destruction. It looked like a war zone.

To make matters worse, there was the aftermath of the storm; the things that didn't happen during the storm but were a direct result of it. There was no power for weeks. Stores and restaurants could not open. People were left with no food, no water, and no supplies. More lives were lost as nursing homes and hospitals were left with no power, no air conditioning, and no refrigeration or electricity that they were depending on to help keep residents and patients alive.

There was a gas shortage. And we can't forget how the levies broke and caused even more damage and loss of lives. Horror stories began to emerge about the rise of crime in certain areas, as some took advantage of a desperate situation. Almost twenty years later, you can still see some of the effects of Hurricane Katrina. Places that were never rebuilt or repaired now lay in waste. Vacant, unused, and desolate.

This is the nature of a storm. It disrupts and dismantles. Storms cause damage on different levels. You can prepare in advance for some storms, but others come without warning. You can't control a storm, but you can make a choice to leave or to ride it out.

Life will create storms of its own. So many times, we become overwhelmed with what is going on in our lives. As wives, we face the pressure of caring for our family, running our households, and tending to our careers. In most cases, that does not include the time needed to care for and tend to ourselves, our health, and our wellbeing. Add to that the pressure of being a caretaker for a spouse that has survived trauma in their past. We can soon find ourselves in the midst of a storm.

It's much like being caught in the eye of a hurricane. In the middle, it seems like nothing is happening (it's actually quite calm and peaceful). But all around you, life is getting caught up in the whirlwind. You can survive a storm. But the key is to have the necessary knowledge and skills you need to survive.

The effects of a storm can be far reaching. You never know how what you are going through may affect other areas or your life. Your relationships can suffer. Your children can be affected. Your health can decline. Some things you go through will have a lasting effect. It can change the way you view the world and the way you see your situation. Trouble and trials can leave you vulnerable, defenseless, and empty on the inside.

Rain can be a good thing. A storm will point out the areas in your life that you need to work on. It will bring out what is truly on the inside. The natural response to a storm is fear. The storm always appears bigger than you. More powerful. Because you are not in control, you lose focus on what is good and magnify in your mind only what is negative. Once you lose your focus, you begin to lose your faith; and when your faith is not present, fear will take over.

Fear binds the mind. It will paralyze you. It will keep you stuck in a place or space that you don't have to be in. Fear will tell you there is no way out, that it's not going to get better, and that things will never change. The goal of fear is to keep you from progress, from purpose, and from fulfilling your potential.

During Katrina, my house was about three blocks from the beach. My front door was facing south, which was the direction of the ocean. The house was hit by that twenty-five-foot storm surge; a big wall of water. There were other houses in the area that were completely wiped off their slab. In fact, after the storm I had a clear view of the ocean from my front door. My house, however, was spared. We did have some flooding, maybe a few feet. Everything on the outside was destroyed, but not one window was broken. The water entered the house through the front door, which I'm sure gave way to the force of the rushing water that seized it. We lost everything on our first floor. However, things were not as bad as they could have been.

You see, there was an old oak tree in front of my house. It was huge. The roots ran deep, and the width of the tree and its limbs almost covered the front of the house. So, when the wall of water came, it had to hit the tree first!!! The water had no choice but to be redirected! This is what saved my house. The tree was anchored. It was the roots that kept it grounded.

Much like that tree, we must be grounded. It is our faith that keeps us anchored. God is a shelter in the storm. We don't have to fear because our confidence is in Him.

"God is our refuge and strength, an ever-present help in trouble. Therefore we will not fear…" (Psalm 46:1-2, NIV).

Where your faith lies, you will find your confidence. Where you have your confidence, you can be at peace. If you have no peace, there is a problem with your faith.

Peace is not the absence of trouble. It is the ability to find the quiet in the midst of the storm. Your faith will give you peace that goes beyond what you can understand. This means that although everything around you may feel like all hell is breaking loose, peace will keep you calm to help you better manage your emotions, your behavior, and your reaction to your circumstances.

Having peace means that you have no inner turmoil or conflict. Peace is found within. It has to do with contentment. This only comes through relationship with Christ. You are content because you know that He has all things under His control. If you are searching for inner peace, that means your spirit is trying to cope with the turmoil that surrounds you.

There are times that trouble comes even when we've done nothing to cause it. So, why does God allow bad things to happen to us? It's all about His permissive will. If He allows something to happen, it's because there is a purpose behind it. He allows it because there is a reason for it. Because it happens in His permissive will, it can only go so far. He won't give you more than you can handle; even though it doesn't always feel that way. Give yourself some credit, everyone doesn't survive what you have been through. But you made it through and are proof that it can be done.

James tells us to "count it all joy" when we encounter troubles and trials of all kinds. To a nonbeliever, this does not make sense. Why would we want to find joy in going through pain and heartache? It is because joy is not dependent on our outward circumstance. It is based on who is at work in us. The power lies with Him, not with us. So, we depend on Him to be that oak standing firm when the waters come rushing in. Yes, we may get wet, but we won't drown.

The Word says we should cast our cares upon Him because He cares for us. "Come unto me, all you who are weary and burdened, and I will give you rest" (Matthew 11:28, NIV). He wants to help you when you are carrying the weight of the world. We were not meant to do it on our own. The verse goes on to say that His way is easy. This is because He has already won the battle. We just need to walk in the victory He has already given us.

Jesus says in John 16:33, "In this world you will have trouble. But take heart! I have overcome the world" (NIV). Isn't that comforting? Jesus was letting us know that He is greater than any challenge we may face. By putting our faith and focus on Him, we take the power away from the negative circumstances in our lives. When we take the power from it, it no longer has control over us. God has already worked it out and He is turning it around to work for your good.

Being content is based on your faith and your confidence in Him. The only way to survive the trouble of this world is to have faith in the creator, protector, and savior of it. Contentment means remembering that the joy of the Lord is your strength. Joy is not dependent on outside circumstances. "Delight yourself in the Lord, and He will give you the desires of your heart" (Psalm 37:4, ESV). To delight yourself means to find joy in Him and His ways. You will find that the desires of your heart will soon look like the desires of His heart. What you want will become what He desires for you to have or do.

As a PTSD Wife, you can experience your own storms in the form of trauma. This can be added to the trauma of your own past. It can also connect to the pain that has kept you bound. You can begin to feel sorry for yourself and become addicted to your story.

Do you want to be free?

Start by breaking the cycle. To change what you do, you have to learn to change the way you think. Mindset is everything. Put things in order. When you put God first, everything else will fall in line. Lean into God and learn His ways.

Isolation and loneliness can be used at times for protection. It's like a defense mechanism. Personal pain can affect your relationships; even those outside of your marriage. We were created to connect with one another. When we are in pain, we think no one can understand what we are going through.

Take a moment and reflect. What are you going through? If trauma is at the root, what fruit has it produced in your life? Where in your life can you see the results of the trauma you have experienced or are experiencing now?

Stop going back to the pain. Consider what it is costing you to stay in that place of hurt and disappointment. Pain will try to tell you who you are. You are not what you have been through. And you are certainly not what you are going through in this moment. You are a survivor and an overcomer. Pain will try to change your identity. It is not enough just to survive because you are left with the memory and emotional scars. You need to overcome the pain of your past and the pain you are experiencing now.

Peace is a Fruit of the Spirit (Galatians 5:22-23). Fruit takes time to grow and to be harvested. It takes work. The Word says we must pursue peace. We must go after it. Be intentional and seek after it. The Fruit of the Spirit is the evidence of His presence in your life. It shows that He is there and at work in you.

You must stay connected to God. Learn to see Him as the Source of everything you need. But even more than that, get to know Him as a Father; your Heavenly Father who loves and cares for you. Fix your focus on Him. Everything else is a distraction.

It is just as important to seek peace with others (especially in marriage) as it is to seek peace for yourself. When your relationship is good, you are good. When you are good, it reflects in your relationship. One thing affects the other.

Storms won't last forever. Eventually, dark grey skies will give way to the sun as a new beginning is always on the horizon. You need to know that God will keep you safe and sound as you learn to depend on Him. He will help you find inner peace, self-love, and personal strength to help you survive your storm. Be still and know that He is God.

"God is within her, she will not fall; God will help her at break of day" (Psalm 46:5, NIV).

Chapter 3: Let's Talk About Trauma

PTSD is Post Traumatic Stress Disorder. Trauma is a response to an event or moment that has already ended; a natural disaster (like a tornado or an earthquake), an accident, mass shooting, rape, abuse, just to name a few. You can be traumatized by being a witness, even if the actual event did not happen directly to you. It is a result of being put in a situation where a person's own life or physical wellbeing (or that of a loved one) is in danger. The effect that trauma can have on a person can go well beyond the moment that it happened. It can continue for years, even a lifetime if it is never addressed and treated.

In that person's mind, the event lives on. They live in a constant state of fear. The memory of a past event can keep them stuck in their mind in that moment. They may be easily triggered, experiencing flashbacks and nightmares. When a person deals with that kind of emotional turmoil, they can react in several different ways.

Essentially, what they want is a sense of control and security. The trauma has taught them just the opposite; that they are not in control, they are not safe, and there is no sense of security for them. This can cause one to lash out on others in anger, or withdraw to themselves in isolation. They may self-medicate with drugs, alcohol, sex, or other self-destructive behavior.

PTSD is normally accompanied by depression (hopelessness), anxiety (fear/worry about the unknown), and guilt or shame. Relationships can suffer because all areas of life (both personal and professional) can be affected. It is relationships with those that are closest to them that suffer the most.

As a PTSD Wife, you will often feel that you are the target of all the negative energy. Afterall, it is those that are closest to us that hurt us the most. You may begin to question or doubt your decision to be with this person. You may even experience a trauma or have symptoms of PTSD of your own. Being a caretaker can often wear on you mentally and cause you emotional stress.

While PTSD is a legitimate medical condition, there is also a spiritual aspect to it. Everything and everyone is governed by a spirit. The way a person acts, speaks, and thinks are all driven by a spirit. Matthew 7 talks about how you can determine what type of tree it is by the fruit that it bears. Good fruit is pleasant to the eye. It is desirable. It tastes good and is easy to digest. Bad fruit may look good from a distance and may even taste good, but give it time, you will not be able to digest it and it may even make you sick. If you want to know the type of spirit you are dealing with, check out the fruit. You can identify it by the effect that it produces.

Have you ever been in a good mood and then someone walks in the room and the energy changes? They may draw you into an argument and before you know it, you are angry or yelling and crying. Or have you experienced the opposite? Have you ever been around someone that can make you feel better when you are in their presence? They can change the way you feel with a smile, or with their conversation, or simply just by their presence.

When a person goes through trauma, there may be physical pain, but that will eventually go away. It is the emotional pain of the experience that will last longer and can do more damage. The way that a person acts and responds in certain situations is a direct result of what they have learned in their past experience and what they know to be true.

Trauma plants a poisonous seed and over time, it begins to take root and bear fruit.

Have you ever seen the movie, *Little Shop of Horrors*? It's a musical based on the stage play. It's the story of a man that finds a strange and exotic plant. He takes the plant in and begins to care for it. He soon finds out that the plant will only eat human blood. The more he eats, the bigger he gets. At first, the man pricks his own fingers and feeds the plant with his own blood. But soon he finds the plant is not satisfied with that and wants more. Eventually, the man resorts to killing people to feed the hungry plant. When the man first took the plant in, he was in a tiny pot. By the end of the movie, the plant took up the whole room and had sprouted tiny mini Audrey 2s (which is what the man named the plant).

This is exactly what trauma does when you allow it to take root. At first, you may miss the signs or overlook the fact that there is a problem. It may seem as if it is no big deal. Blood is a life source, which means you need it to survive. Much like the effects of trauma, the plant began to drain the man of his life source. Trauma will drain your peace. It will take your joy. It will strip you of all hope, and you will eventually lose faith. When you lose your faith, you begin to die a spiritual death. You'll be alive on the outside but cold and numb on the inside. The Bible calls it having a heart of stone.

Proverbs 4:23 tells us to guard our hearts. We should watch over it and protect it. Why? Because it is the source of life. The function of the heart is to pump the blood to circulate through your body. It gives life to your entire body, including your organs that keep you alive. If the heart were to stop working, the body could not sustain, and death would soon follow. The same is true in the spirit.

God wants us to have a pure heart (1 Timothy 1:5). He wants us to love Him, to pursue relationship with Him. He also wants us to love one another, to show love and compassion to each other, always putting others first and seeking the greater good. Because God is love (1 John 4:8), a heart of stone or a heart without love is a heart without God.

It is your heart that reveals what is really going on within, where you are emotionally, and what you believe. It governs your thoughts, your actions, and your intentions. The heart controls the mind. The mind controls the actions of the body, the things you say and the things you do.

Trauma can take your heart and shatter it into a million tiny little pieces. When your heart is in pieces, your soul is in pieces. Remember Humpty Dumpty? He was broken and no one could figure out how to put him back together again. And that was the end of the story. Apparently, he spent the rest of his life broken. One thing the story does not reveal is how Humpty Dumpty fell. Did he make a mistake? Did someone push him? Was he dropped?

We will never be in control of everything that happens in our life. There are some things that are out of our control. There are some situations and some pain we must go through because of the actions of others.

I'd like to introduce you to Mephibosheth.

Mephibosheth was the son of King Saul. When the kingdom was overthrown, his father and grandfather were killed. As the news hit the palace, his nurse picked him up to flee from the danger and in her haste, she fell and ended up dropping him, crippling both of his feet. He was five years old.

Years later, we find Mephibosheth living in LoDebar. The name literally means "No pasture. No word. No communication." It was a dry place. There was no life there. No growth and no hope. It seemed like a place where people or things go to die.

Mephibosheth was royalty. I would imagine that living in the palace, he had access to everything that he would ever need or desire. But like many, he had a traumatic experience, and at such a young age. He had his whole life before him. He was royalty from a long line of tall, good-looking men who fought in and led the army. But tragedy struck, and in an instant, he lost his family, his home, and with the damage done to his body, he lost all hope of the future that was planned for him.

What happened to him was not his fault. He was not in control of the situation on that fateful day. He was under the care of his nurse. She had good intentions. Her plan was to save his life. But because she stumbled and dropped him, her actions changed his life forever.

We have all been dropped. Somewhere down the line, someone that was supposed to love and care for us stumbled and dropped us. It could be a relationship that ended, or a loved one that passed away. It could be due to neglect or abuse. There are so many things that have happened that changed the life of those connected to them. You can also be dropped by life, not necessarily by a loved one. Life can let you down. It is important to know that it is not your fault. So many times, we say, "If only this would not have happened, or if he wouldn't have done this, then I could be so much happier, or better off, or I would not be in this place…"

Being dropped can leave you feeling vulnerable and unfulfilled. It can damage your self-esteem and make you question or doubt your self-worth. You may struggle with guilt and shame. Your past can keep you paralyzed. Just like in LoDebar, there will be no growth, no progress, and no moving forward.

Think about water that has been left stagnant. Just sitting there with no movement. Harmful toxic bacteria builds over time. There is an odor, mosquitos and undesirables are attracted, and the fish are unable to survive, so they die. The effects of trauma are the same. There is no life, and you can become toxic.

Stagnant water stinks! It is a sign to let people know that something is wrong and not to go near it. When you've been dropped, your behavior and the way you relate to other people can be a turnoff and act as a repellent to keep people away. You become host to parasites like fear, depression, anger, and guilt.

This is LoDebar.

The residents of LoDebar know exactly where they live. It's not that they would not mind living somewhere else. In this case, the grass IS greener on the other side. The problem is that either they don't know how or don't have the energy to find their way out. They have become complacent and have accepted the idea that they are just stuck there.

The key to leaving LoDebar is to come out first with your mind. You must change your mindset by changing your focus. It starts with a thought. If you want to change your life, start by changing your mind. Sounds easy, doesn't it? Change does not come until YOU put in the work. It is not easy. The longer you have been doing a thing, the harder it is to come out of it. Change requires consistency, persistence, and a will to keep going no matter what, until you reach your goal. Change happens first in your mind.

Did you know your mind is so powerful that it can change the trajectory of your life? That is why it is a target of the enemy. It is prime real estate. Where the mind goes, the body will follow. Most abusers have figured this out. If you want to control a person, you have to get in their mind first. You have to change the way they think, make them think that your voice or opinion is the only one that matters. You must also make them insecure about who they are. Once you do this, it is easy to control them.

This is what the enemy does. He whispers toxic thoughts and ideas into our heads, and if we are not careful and allow it, they will seep in and become our own thoughts and reality. Peter warns us, "Be sober minded, be alert. Your adversary the devil is prowling around like a roaring lion, looking for anyone he can devour" (1 Peter 5:8).

When you don't have control over your mind, it is like a city with no walls. There are no boundaries and no protection. Nothing to keep you safe. You are vulnerable. The process of healing your mind is a spiritual thing.

Paul teaches that our struggle is not against flesh and blood, but against the rulers, against the authorities, against the cosmic powers of this darkness, against evil, spiritual forces in the heavens.

I know, I know. It sounds spooky and supernatural; like the set up for a great action-adventure movie. But think about it. Every word, every thought, every action is governed by a spirit. Paul breaks it down for us in Romans 8:5 "For those who live according to the flesh have their minds set on the things of the flesh, but those who live according to the Spirit have their minds set on the things of the Spirit. Now the mindset of the flesh is death, but the mindset of the Spirit is life and peace."

When you are in LoDebar, your mindset is that of the flesh. It leads to death; the death of your spirit, your peace, and your joy. The only way out of LoDebar is to be transformed by the renewing of your mind (Romans 12:2).

Chapter 4: The Elephant in the Room

The fifth chapter of Mark begins with a story about Jesus's encounter with one who is described as a madman. He had an "unclean spirit." To begin with, the man had been living among the tombs in the graveyard among the dead. It goes on to describe how no one had been able to restrain him. He broke through the chains and ropes they had tried to shackle him with trying to subdue him. It says no one was strong enough to control him. The man spent his days and nights among the tombs on the mountains, always crying out and cutting himself with stones.

The story does not go into detail about how the man ended up in this condition, only that he had an unclean spirit. What I noticed is that it says that no one could subdue him. They could not control him. This tells me that it was his choice to live among the tombs. Since he could not be controlled, he made the decision to live there.

Why would someone choose to live among the dead? Perhaps his breaking point was the death of a loved one. Maybe the situation was too much for him to handle. Overcome by grief, depression, and perhaps unresolved anger about the situation, the man began to sink into an emotional abyss, plunging into darkness to a place of no hope and great despair.

Whenever the Bible talks about a person that has an "unclean spirit," it is referring to the fact that the person is under a spiritual attack and being mentally controlled by a demonic force, which determines their behavior. Now don't let this scare you. I'm sure someone is reading this and visualizing that movie where the girl's head began to spin, and she started spitting pea soup. That's Hollywood (or HollyWeird, as my dad used to call it). That is not reality. In real life, a demonic possession is a case of the "I can't help its." This is not to be confused with the habits we struggle to break. That is different.

Demonic possession is usually brought on by a weakness or an opening we have in our soul. In the case of trauma, your soul becomes vulnerable because you are at a weakened emotional state. As mentioned earlier, the devil is already talking to you and trying to take over your mind using his tactics of lies and persuasion.

You often hear in the news how people plead guilty by insanity, where they claim the voices in their head told them to do something hurtful to someone. When you talk of depression that leads to suicidal thoughts, that is a mental health issue. When you talk about the shedding of innocent blood, ESPECIALLY that of CHILDREN, you are no longer dealing with a health issue. That is pure evil. This is a spiritual problem.

Demonic possession can be self-inflicted as well. It can be allowed in by your own actions and permission. Have you ever noticed that most liquor stores have the phrase "Wine and Spirits" as a part of their branding? A mind under the influence of drugs and alcohol is actually under the control of the substance they've put in their body. That's why they start hallucinating and seeing things. They hear voices and are unable to control their behavior. Their emotions become entangled, and they get extremely sensitive because they cannot control their emotions. This leads to an emotional outpour like crying, arguing, explosive outbursts, and even physical fights.

Proverbs chapter 20 says wine is a mocker and strong drink is a brawler. In other words, it can encourage you to make a fool of yourself and even start fights. Anything that can alter your mental state of mind to make you lose control is simply an open door to allow an "unclean spirit" to come in and take possession of your mind.

We've been conditioned to think that there is no harm in "having a little something" to relax or to "take the edge off." Some use it as a way of escape to get their mind off their reality that they must soon face once they come down from their high.

Survivors of trauma have a constant need to escape from reality because their past is always haunting them. This can lead to self-destructive behaviors that can affect more than just the person that is partaking in the activity. Often, it is the people that love them, and that are closest to them that feel the brunt of these actions.

The man at the tomb, at one point, had people that cared enough to try to help him. He was obviously in turmoil and dealing with emotional distress. He was inconsolable, behaving erratically, and trying to harm himself. I don't believe he was suicidal. Cutting himself with the rocks seemed to be a coping mechanism for him to express his pain.

If someone is hurting themselves, common sense says to remove the threat to avoid further damage. So, what did they do? They tried to restrain him by binding his hands and feet. Perhaps first with rope and when that did not work, then with chains. But that didn't work either. The man seemed to have superhuman strength that was accredited to the demon possession.

There are news stories about how people under the influence of certain drugs have had this same kind of power. What is really happening is in their mind, they are hallucinating and paranoid, having an out-of-body experience. Adrenaline kicks in and they get this extraordinary strength, much like it does with a mom that lifts a car to save her baby.

I can imagine those that cared about the man grew weary of trying to help him. No matter what they did, he was not receptive to their attempts. He couldn't be. He was not in his right mind, so they did what everyone else had done. They left him alone to his madness.

I imagine that this was not easy for them. Seeing a loved one in pain and not being able to do anything about it is heartbreaking in and of itself. It can take a toll on that loved one. They may have to deal with their own battle of depression and other issues based on their perceived failure to help them.

Cases of divorce associated with PTSD have a very high percentage rate, especially in military families. Trust issues, problems with intimacy and communication, as well as loss of interest in being social can contribute to relationship problems. Add to that the effects of self-medicating substance abuse and there you will find a recipe for disaster.

The problem is that families are not equipped to handle the changes and challenges brought on by the effects of trauma. Just as in the story, it's easier to leave them to their own madness than to continue in dysfunction. PTSD affects the whole household.

Addiction is a type of spiritual slavery. The bottom line is that your spouse is hurting. They use the substance to regulate their emotions. They get hooked on it and this creates the addiction. Addiction kills relationships. It becomes the focus. They want to feed it. The addiction stands in place of a valid need. You must get to the root. This should be the target of your prayers and your action.

To some extent, they feel guilt and shame because they know they are not in control. Like Jesus, we are to have compassion. "When he saw the crowds, he had compassion on them, because they were harassed and helpless, like sheep without a shepherd" (Matthew 9:36, NIV).

Some are not in a position to help themselves. It's okay to love from a distance. Love covers, but it also corrects. Some may use manipulation by starting fights and making you the bad guy. Misery loves MISERABLE company. They want you to feel as bad as they do. They try to react to get you to leave them alone. They'll have you walking on eggshells as they turn the blame on you. Over time, their condition takes higher precedence than the marriage. Don't get drawn in. Disengage!

Take the pressure off yourself. It is not your job to fix them. This is their own personal fight. Your only job is to support from the sidelines. Hold them accountable. The "I-Can't-Help-Its" (for the most part) are just an excuse. Don't give in to it. Self-destructive behavior needs an intervention. As a spouse, we can be water or fuel to that fire. I said it before, you can't fix them, but you can enable them to stay sick.

There are two types of people involved in a codependent relationship. First, there is the person that is actively engaging in harmful, self-destructive behavior. The other person is the enabler. This is the person that, in some kind of way, is supporting the negative behavior displayed by the first person in our scenario. Usually, codependency centers around cases where people are dealing with issues of substance abuse. A person becomes an enabler by the things that they do and don't do when it comes to dealing with the other person. There's a difference between helping the person and enabling them. If you helping the person makes it easier for them to continue in their destructive behavior, then you are enabling them and causing the problem to get worse.

How do you know if you are an enabler? Do you ignore or tolerate toxic behavior? Are you buying or paying for the substances that the person is abusing, like alcohol or drugs? Do you make excuses for their destructive behavior? Do you avoid confronting the issue just to keep the peace or because you are worried about how they will react to you? Do you let it slide when they say or do harmful or abusive things to you? Do you hold them accountable for their actions? Do you follow through on consequences? Like ACTUALLY leaving when you say you're going to leave? How about neglecting your own needs in order to make sure that they're alright?

Codependency is a learned behavior. It's about how much you let the person get away with. You've heard the saying, "Give them a foot and they'll take a mile." It's true. The more you allow a person to get away with behaving in a negative way toward you, the more they will continue to do it, and in most cases, the worse it will get.

Codependency is a cycle. It actually starts with the person that is allowing the harmful behavior. It is a clear sign that there are no boundaries put in place and if there are, they are not being honored.

So, why would someone allow another person to continue to violate their peace and disrupt their emotional wellbeing?

It's because there is an emotional hole deep down that they are trying to fill. Somewhere down the line, their self-esteem, self-confidence, and self-worth have been violated and bruised. Somewhere deep down inside of a grown woman is a young girl that has been wounded and never got over her fear of rejection and abandonment.

This is why women stay in relationships that are abusive. They get comfortable with what they know. They learn how to maneuver around the relationship just enough to survive. Fear of the unknown can outweigh common sense. In their mind, they are scared to leave because they don't think they can make it without the person. They've become well acquainted with operating in dysfunction. So, they give their permission by the behavior and action they tolerate. They've become used to it. And it becomes their new normal.

If you are in a codependent relationship, it's time to break the cycle. You are meant for so much more. It's time to do the work and start building boundaries. To begin with, cut off the financial support. Don't buy supplies or give them money to support their habit. By you withholding financial support, they will have to become more self-reliant. Let them deal with their own problems. Stop making excuses for them and running to their rescue. Let them deal with the consequences of their own actions. Set your boundaries and stick to them. Once you have gotten to your breaking point, do not go back to the way things were. Establish consequences. Clearly communicate them and stick to it!!

Your position as a PTSD Wife is difficult. It's hard to be in this position dealing with an addiction on top of everything else. You must know how to function in dysfunction and love them through the worst of times. Help them to see the reality of their situation. Realization (or fear) of loss may motivate them to seek help. Let them know what is at stake; their marriage, relationships, jobs, opportunities, and more. They might come to the realization that they need to get it together.

It's okay to be angry. Righteous anger is an anger against sin or that which is not right. Real love steps in and corrects. Remind them that they are better than the way they are behaving; that they are not acting like themselves or the person you married. And let them know that you love them too much to continue to watch them hurt themselves in this way. Don't try to be their parent. Talk to them as their loving wife.

Continually ask God to work in your heart. To help you forgive and to direct you on how to help them and how to be the spouse he needs in that moment. Set a standard for yourself to know what you are willing to accept or not.

Undoing the hurt and pain of your past is a process. It takes time. But you can start right now by protecting your peace, renewing your mind, and establishing boundaries.

Chapter 5: You Are Essential

Women were created with a purpose: To be a help. We were designed to fit a need; to fill in the gap. Now, don't twist this thought. This does not mean that we are not to be supported in our own dreams and endeavors. It doesn't mean that we are beneath or not equal to men. God created the world and then created Adam in His image. He is a triune God, comprised of God the Father, God the Son, and God the Holy Spirit, but that is a conversation for another time…and another book. The trinity is a reflection of relationship in heaven, with all three working together as one. This is what the Lord envisioned for man as He formed Eve from Adam's rib. God saw that with all he had around him, it was not good for man to be alone. He needed someone that will be suitable to help him.

Did you catch that? You were designed to be a suitable help to your spouse. We are all born with purpose and have divine connection, especially in the covenant of marriage. Everything with God is planned, even down to who you marry. There is a purpose for it all. This is not to be confused with His permissive will, as sometimes we do get connected to the wrong person. He has graced us to be able to overcome the challenges that will come our way, no matter the situation. God knew that you would go through certain rough times because of who you are connected to. But He has equipped you with all you need to make it through.

Eve was a solution to Adam's needs, just as you are the solution to your spouse's needs. God did not want Adam to be alone. But why? He needed to fill in the gap where he was lacking and balance him out. The purpose of Eve was to make up for the "deficiencies" that Adam may have had. There are some places your spouse will fall short and not be able to help themselves. It's like that itch you cannot reach. You need someone to help you scratch it. In essence, Eve was created to have Adam's back.

She was equal to him, as she was part of him. "Bone of my bone, flesh of my flesh" (Genesis 2:23). She was created or formed from his rib. The purpose of this was UNITY; working together as one to fulfill the goal. This is what it was all about. There is plenty of opposition on the way to the goal. Just as on a football field, the offense is working to get the ball to the other side. In order to do this, one person runs with the ball while the rest of the team blocks the other players on the opposite team from tackling them. They simply work together to clear the way for the player to make it to the other side. The goal in marriage is to fulfill your purpose so that you can get to what God has promised you.

The enemy uses division to break up the unity of your marriage. There is power in unity. Family is the basic unit of society. If he can divide the family, he can attack the individual, and not the family as a unit. God created marriage. It represents unity and covenant. Your goal is to keep the peace in your union. "Two are better than one because they have a good return for their labor: If either of them falls down, one can help the other up…though one be overpowered, two can defend themselves. A cord of three strands is not easily broken" (Ecclesiastes 4:9-10, CSB).

A PTSD spouse is called to stand in the gap. Your job is to support and defend. Hold them up where they are weak. Love them through when they fall short. Marriage is the true definition of "I've got your back."

You are a helper, you were designed to suit the needs of your spouse. You were created to fit perfectly with them. At the time you were formed in your mother's belly, you were already the answer to the problems and challenges your spouse would face. You were already equipped and capable of satisfying their needs. You have been graced and anointed for your marriage to be exactly who they need you to be.

Your role as a wife and mother is to protect your family at all costs. You are a spiritual covering for them. As your husband leads the family, you are to cover him as well. Your prayers for him are key to a successful family life. You want to pray for his health and his strength, for his decision-making process, for his circle of friends and associates, and by all means, pray for his spirit and his emotional wellbeing.

As the wife, you are the one that is closest to him. You know him well; when he is up and when he is down, when he is weak and when he is strong. Your connection should be so that you can step in to ease the burden when you sense he needs it. You are a team, one in mind and spirit. You balance each other out.

You must always stay on guard and ready for action. In the Bible, cities were surrounded by tall walls for protection. They were called fortified cities. There was usually someone assigned to sit on the wall to look for oncoming danger and surprise enemy attacks so they could sound the alarm. As the wife, this is your responsibility; to watch for those signs of danger and sound the alarm so the Lord will fight your battle.

Stay on guard. When you notice that something is "off" with your husband, address it right away. Not in an accusatory or combative way, but in love. Ask him how he's doing. Try to get him involved in conversation. Listen closely. Not just to what he is saying, but also listen to the things he is NOT saying. Learn how to read between the lines. This is where intimacy comes in. You must understand and know how to connect to the spirit of your loved one.

Our job is to make our home a safe haven for him (and the rest of the family); a place of peace. Home is where you are. YOU are the safe haven for him. He fights all day in the world for respect; to be treated with dignity. He fights daily for his place in the world. Everything outside the doors of your home tells him who he is not. It is your job to tell him who he IS. At home, he should not have to prove his worth because there he is already valued.

Trauma can affect a person on many levels. The bottom line is their sense of security has been stripped away from them. Trauma first happens in the physical. There is a part of the body that experiences pain, loss, or injury. In most cases, the actual event has ended. It has already happened, and the person is no longer in danger. But trauma also affects a person on a mental level. These effects can be long lasting as the memory lives on. A person can be stuck in that same moment and that same time, especially if they encounter something that triggers the memory of that event. Trauma can also affect one's trust, which is connected to their faith. They may become spiritually dead inside, numb to the world. This can lead to them walking away from God and can in turn lead to depression and other conditions of the heart and mind.

This is why your role as a wife is so important. Everyone needs someone in their corner to help them to stand, or fight, when they cannot do it for themselves. Yes, there are some battles that they will have to fight on their own, as there are some things that only God can do. Remember, it is not your job to fix them. But you can definitely be the support they need to help them along the way.

There is a story in the Bible that talks about how four men were trying to get their friend to Jesus. The man was paralyzed and had no way to get to Jesus on his own. They had enough faith to know that if they could just get him to Jesus, He could heal the man. They were persistent. They were not able to reach Him by just walking in the door. He was teaching and the crowd surrounding him was great. There was no room to get the man to Him, so they climbed to the top of the building and lowered him through the roof. This was a testament of their faith. They knew where his help had to come from and believed they had to get their friend to Jesus by any means necessary.

Just like those friends, we as wives have to be willing to carry our spouse to Jesus when they do not have the will, the fight, the drive, or the energy to do it for themselves. How do we do this? Through prayer. We intercede for them. Intercession builds a bridge. It is the act of bringing two sides together. In this case, you are bringing your husband to the Lord to ask for His help and maybe to intervene in a certain situation.

When you pray for change remember that change happens from within. You don't pray to change the situation because there are some things you will have to go through in order to grow in faith and knowledge, and increase your strength. Your request should not be for God to change them. They have to be a willing participant in their own change. Pray instead that God will change you for the situation. Ask for revelation and a plan, how you should proceed. Ask Him what to do and what NOT to do.

Prayer is a weapon, especially when you use it in conjunction with the Word of God. Learn to soak your prayers with the Word. You can't use the Word if you don't know it. Find out what the Word has to say about what you are going through. Who in the Bible went through a similar situation? How did God change the outcome? What promises does the Bible make for doing things HIS way? How can you apply this to what you are going through now? Trust me, your answer is in there! Once you have the information, then you can pray what the Bible says and just watch God work!

Romans 8:34 tells us that Jesus intercedes for us. And just before that in verse 26, we learn that sometimes we don't know what we need to pray for, so the Holy Spirit intercedes for us…covering us in that spot we cannot reach. Just like Him, we should also intercede for our spouse, as there may be times when they cannot come to God on their own behalf. Like us at times, they may not know what it is they need to be praying for. Intercession is not just a prayer. It is an activity. It is our faith in action. You can pray a prayer of intercession. The Holy Spirit builds a bridge for us and connects us to God's will. He wants to carry the burden for you, and that is what prayer will do. It transfers the burden and lightens your load.

Learn how to pray and **leave it there**!! Ask God to intervene on their behalf. Prayer is comprised of four main elements. **Petition** – Ask God for what you desire or stand in need of. **Repent** – Ask for forgiveness for the sins or offenses that keep you separated from God (and each other), and then change the behavior. **Acknowledge** – Recognize God as the source of all your needs, from whom all blessings flow. And finally, **Yield** – Accept and submit to His will. He has the final say.

Be persistent and be patient. Some things take time! When you plant the seed, there is a certain amount of time that must go by before you can reap the harvest. This time in between is the process. You can't skip the process. You have to go through some things to perfect your faith and build your faith in God.

Have faith. He can do it all! It is not a matter of CAN He do it. But WILL He do it? What if He doesn't? The truth is our way may not be His way. He would never withhold a good thing from us, but He will not release it until it is time for Him to do so. Sometimes the answer is "No." We may never understand why He allows us to go through certain things. Maybe He wants to build or increase something in us or bring us closer to Him. He knows and He understands. He has already answered before you ask. The waiting period, or the process, is your season for development. Watch for your prayers to be answered. No matter how small. Your faith is under attack! If you give up hope, you will stop fighting. Your prayers have purpose and they are what is helping to bring your spouse out of LoDebar. He reminds us that His strength is made perfect in our weakness. God is able to do more than we can ask or think. And that's a promise!!

Chapter 6: Start the Battle

When you really want something in life you have to fight for it. The harder you have to work for something, the more value it holds and the least likely you will be to let it go or to mismanage it. Your mind is the most precious possession you could ever own. It houses your emotions, your will, your intellect, your memories, desires, and more. Something so valuable needs to be protected. Why? Because it is always going to be a target of the enemy.

Do you remember Indiana Jones? I love those movies. He was a college professor of archeology, dressed in a suit and tie. But he was also a legendary action hero who would narrowly escape death and danger as he went on great adventures to find the most prized of possessions.

In each movie, once he got to the treasure, he couldn't just walk up to it and get it. He had to go through the most dangerous obstacle course full of tricks and traps. From all the skeletons along the way, you can tell that many tried but failed. The way they guarded the treasures in these movies is the way we should guard our minds. Don't make it easy for the enemy. Because the battleground is your mind, you will need to be ready for the fight.

Paul tells us in Ephesians that we need to put on the Armor of God so that we can resist (or protect ourselves from) the enemy (Ephesians 6:13). The rest of the scripture goes into great detail about each piece of the Armor of God. In this chapter we will focus on one piece in particular; the sword. You cannot come out of LoDebar without a fight, and every warrior needs a great weapon.

Fun fact about me, I am a Marvel nerd. I love superheroes, action movies, and a great fight scene. In my opinion, no one does it better than Marvel's Black Widow (that is until her sister showed up). Black Widow is known for her precision and skill, and mastery of weapons. But it's not just that. She does it with such style and swag and it looks like second nature to her. I once read a book that said she was trained so well that her body became the weapon and anything she picked up was simply an extension of her body.

This is what we need to do with our mind; turn our mind into a weapon. How do we do that? I'm glad you asked! By picking up the sword: The Word of God!

"For the Word of God is alive and active. Sharper than any double-edged sword, it penetrates even to dividing the soul and spirit, joints, and marrow; it judges the thoughts and attitudes of the heart" (Hebrews 4:12).

What does this mean? It means that God's Word still has power. It is alive and active, which means that it is still working and applicable to every place in our life, every situation we go through, every struggle we face, and every burden we carry in our hearts and on our minds. It is so precise that it can draw a line between your spirit and your soul, and the joint from the marrow. It is a mirror that shows you the truth of what is inside of you. Dividing day from night, wrong from right, it judges the thoughts and the intentions of your heart.

2 Timothy 3:16 says, "All scripture is inspired by God and is profitable for teaching, for rebuking, for correcting, for training in righteousness, so that the man of God may be complete, equipped for every good work."

Not only is it a weapon, but it is also a super tool. Multipurposed, multifunctional. You can use the Word to heal your mind, to build you up, to clean up your act, and to fight the lies of the enemy with its truth. No matter what you are going through in life, you can find help for what you need in the pages of the book. It is also a handbook for life. The answers are right there, you only need to go find them.

Arm yourself with the Word by gathering scripture that helps you to fight those negative thoughts and emotions that keep you bound in LoDebar. It is truth that makes you free. When you are free in your mind, the body will follow.

Learn how to find yourself in the Word. Whatever you are facing in life can be found right there on the pages He gave us. Someone in the Bible has gone through the same issue you are facing now. Find some scriptures to combat what you are feeling. The Bible warns you not to trust your heart because your heart can be deceitful. I can hear what you are thinking… "Ummm, didn't you just tell me to guard my heart? Why would I protect it if it is deceitful?"

Your heart is deceiving because it is connected to your emotions. Your emotions are connected to your mind. As I said, your mind is under constant attack from the enemy who will lie and convince you to feel a certain way which leads you to act based on how you feel. This is never a good thing. You must protect your heart because your emotions will pull you into such a dark place that you will begin to die a slow, spiritual death.

The citizens of LoDebar have all but given up. Their heart has been governed by their emotions and they have accepted that there is no way out. Therefore, you need the truth of the Word. The truth in God's Word will break down the strongholds of the enemy and will set you free in your mind and in your heart. Then and only then will you be able to come out of LoDebar.

As you begin to read, study, and increase your knowledge and understanding of what God says, you will learn how to apply it to your life and then, out of your mouth, declare what the Lord has to say about your situation. Your faith is the driving force of the Rhema, or spoken Word of God. The Holy Spirit will grab that word and move on it. God says in Isaiah 55:11 that His Word will not return to Him void. It will accomplish what He sent it out to do.

Sometimes it is necessary to break away from something or someone for a period of time to take time for yourself and to hear from God. Fasting is a practice in discipline. It is a way to subdue your flesh (your physical nature) and refresh your spirit by reconnecting to God.

Most times, people relate fasting to food, but it is not limited to just that. You can fast from anything. Ideally, you should fast from anything that you have become too dependent on. Food is a given. We have to eat. But, what about social media? The time spent on social media daily is astounding. How many times during the day do you pick up your phone to check it, just out of habit? Sometimes I catch myself checking my phone within a minute of the last time I checked it. We must be careful of the things we come to be dependent on.

This is the purpose of fasting. To break the habits and patterns that keep us bound. Oh yes, if I am checking my phone every minute, I am bound to it. Fasting will break the chains of those things that are binding you.

When you are in LoDebar, you are bound in your mind. Bound to your past, bound to fear, bound to your pain. Thoughts and visions will invade your mind. These are unwanted, uninvited guests in your head, in your personal space. These thoughts and emotions you are experiencing can lead to undesirable behavior and your actions can inflict harm on yourself or others.

There was a man in the Bible who brought his son to Jesus. The child was being tormented by a demonic spirit. It made the child mute, which means he could not talk and he also could not hear. Since childhood, the spirit caused the boy to have violent seizures.

But not only that, the father said the spirit would often try to drown the boy or to throw him in the fire. In other words, the boy was suicidal.

He was tormented by the demons. Not being able to talk or hear and having these seizures diminished his quality of life. He wasn't born this way. The man told Jesus his son had been like that since he was a child (not since birth). That means that everything was fine until one day when it wasn't. Somewhere down the line, he had a traumatic experience. They don't disclose what it was, but from the story you can pinpoint that it happened to him as a young child.

It was very clear that this child was not in control of his body. He suffered, not only from seizures, but he lost the essential functions needed for him to communicate with the world around him. LoDebar was also known as a place of no communication. Imagine not being able to speak or to hear. The frustration he must have felt when trying to communicate. He couldn't receive from the world around him a word of hope or encouragement. You can tell from the text that the father loved him and spent a lot of time with him. But in his mind, the boy could not receive that. There was a constant reminder in his mind that there was something wrong with him and he was powerless to do anything about it.

One of the tricks that the enemy uses is the power of suggestion and persuasion. He uses your mind and thoughts to whisper suggestions, hoping that you will take the bait. The goal of the enemy is to get you to stop believing and to lose your faith. The tactics he uses are to steal, kill, and destroy (John 10:10). In this case, he stole the boy's functions, destroyed his life, and was trying to kill him.

After a traumatic event, your mind is vulnerable. In most cases, the trauma came on unexpectedly, without enough time to prepare for it, physically or mentally. As the saying goes, your mind is all over the place. You have to deal with the memory of what happened, as well as the fear of it happening again. You may develop trust issues or a deep sense of insecurity. Anxiety may keep you in a state of constant panic and awareness. All those emotions at one time can be overwhelming and cause severe emotional stress, which can lead to depression. This will spill out into your relationships and can cause division and isolation. Depression can lead you down a dark path where there is no peace or hope in sight.

I believe this is where this lad was, mentally in a state of severe depression. As I said before, all of our thoughts and actions are motivated by a spirit. It was that spirit that made the boy suicidal, whispering suggestions to his mind. Remember, the boy is both deaf and blind. It was a trick of the enemy to make him believe that it would be better to end it all. The father knew that he was dealing with a spiritual problem, therefore, he knew he needed a spiritual solution. This is why he brought him to Jesus.

You will have to go back and read the full story so you can get the full effect of what happened. Long story short, the disciples tried to heal the boy, but failed, so they brought him to Jesus and He healed him. Later, the disciples asked Jesus why they were not able to cast out the demon and Jesus explained that only prayer and fasting will get rid of this type of demon.

Why do you think this is? Are there certain things that can only be fixed by prayer and fasting? Absolutely! Here's why. When you pray and fast, your body is totally under submission to the Lord; body and soul. Your body is under submission because you are physically denying something, whether it is food, social media, or anything else. Your soul (which houses your mind, your will, your intellect, and your emotions) is under subjection to the Word of God. It is the Word that cleanses your soul, removing what is not like God and replacing it with the truth and power you need to build you up and prepare you for what is next in your life.

The Word is designed to be multifunctional; used in various ways. Of course, you have to read it, accept it, and learn how to apply it to your everyday life. But you will also need to learn how to wield it and harness the power that it gives you. Remember, the Word is a weapon, but it cannot be effective until you release it out of your mouth.

I cannot express the importance of your faith while on this journey. You must believe in something. LoDebar is a place of no Word, no communication. That means you will not be able to hear from God because your heart is not open to receive it. God wants to give you a new spirit (Ezekiel 36:26) and change your heart of stone to a heart of flesh; a heart that will love, laugh, and live again.

A heart trapped in LoDebar is a prisoner, bound by emotional pain and memories of the past. The goal of the enemy is to keep you stuck in this mindset so that you will be ineffective and unable to fulfill your divine purpose. While God did not cause your pain, He did allow it to happen. Nothing happens in this life that will catch God off guard. He is not surprised by anything because He knows all. He sees all. No matter the situation you are going through, there is always a bigger picture involved. That means that your pain, your experience, and the after effects you are feeling now serve a purpose. It is not to hurt you. It is to direct your path. That path leads right to Him.

In the beginning, God's plan was then and has always been for us to fellowship with Him, to build a relationship and a dependence on Him. At the root of this desire for relationship is one true fact: "I have loved you with an everlasting love; therefore, I have continued to extend faithful love to you" (Jeremiah 31:3, CSB).

God loves you. Always has. Always will.

The hurt, pain, and disappointment you feel helps the enemy to cloud your mind and feed you the wrong ideas about God's role in your life. He has promised not to leave you or forsake you. The Lord is near to the brokenhearted; he saves those crushed in spirit (Psalm 34:18, CSB).

Doesn't that sound like the citizens of LoDebar?

In Matthew 11, Jesus invites us to relationship with Him. "Come unto me, all of you who are weary and heavy burdened and I will give you rest. Take up my yoke and learn from me because I am lowly and humble in heart and you will find rest for your souls. For my yoke is easy and my burden is light."

God knew we would need His help. He freely gave it to us in the form of a Savior. Jesus did more than just die on the cross for us. He lifted the weight of burden off of us. Emotional stress can weigh you down. In fact, what goes on in the mind can affect the body. This is why people get ulcers, high blood pressure, headaches, obesity, heart disease, diabetes, cancer, and so much more.

When you are in LoDebar, because you are in a state of mental decline, you are not considering what this is doing to your body. You may feel powerless to do anything about it, or you may not care to do anything about it. This is how a spiritual death can lead to a physical death. But God wants us to have life and have it in abundance (John 10:10). He has a plan for you.

"For I know the plans I have for you. Plans for your wellbeing, not for disaster to give you a future and a hope. You will call to me and come and pray to me and I will listen to you. You will seek me and find me when you search for me with all your heart. I will be found by you..." (Jeremiah 29:11-14).

God's plan all along has been the restoration of relationships. He wants to make you whole by putting back together the pieces of your brokenness. Once you have been made whole again, you can begin to work on mending other parts of your life that may have come undone while in LoDebar.

Chapter 7: Hard to Love

Studies show that 70 percent of marriages dealing with PTSD end in divorce. The truth is, PTSD affects the whole house, not just the person that has experienced the trauma. Marital relationships can become extremely volatile. The smallest disagreement can become an all-out explosive showdown. Rates of divorce, abuse, and violence are much higher in families that are dealing with PTSD. It is not because of irreconcilable differences, or not being able to get along. PTSD can cause a divide in the relationship. Trust issues, misdirected or mishandled anger, and more time spent apart are all issues that a household can experience.

Hostility and conflict can tear a family apart. There can be no growth in a hostile environment. PTSD attacks your marriage in one particular area. Which area is that? I'm glad you asked! It's your connection!! The goal of the enemy is to kill, steal, and destroy. How does he do that? He divides and conquers. The problem is that families are not equipped to handle the changes and challenges brought on by the effects of trauma.

PTSD is NOT the source of all your relationship problems. It highlights the issues that are already present in your relationship. Unmet expectations, selfishness, and misunderstanding can all be valid reasons for their anger. They may have good reason to be upset, but because of the condition of their mind in that moment, especially if it is fueled by alcohol or drugs, it can make matters worse. They will not be open to communicate with you. At this point, their only goal is to get it off their chest.

Let's face it. It can happen. In the heat of the moment, we can lose our cool and be drawn into a fight. Emotions can run high and hot. Your feelings can get the best of you and pretty soon you'll find yourself on a runaway train destined for disaster. There are some things that cannot be taken back once they are released into the atmosphere. Reckless words and actions in that moment can change the course of the relationship forever.

In a battle, the objective is to win, to overpower the opponent in a crushing defeat. To shut them down, no matter the cost. Oftentimes, when dealing with a loved one suffering from PTSD, constant conflict will feel just like this. Hurt people hurt people. They want you to feel and experience the same kind of pain they are feeling. When a person is in such an emotional state, there is no limit. They are blinded by rage and lashing out to release the anger and frustration that has been building up inside.

The key to handling conflict is to first try your best not to get involved. There is wisdom and power in staying silent. It prevents you from creating more problems and doing more damage. "The one who guards his mouth and tongue keeps himself out of trouble" (Proverbs 21:23, CSB). If you see a situation turning, simply walk away. Choose to end the conversation. Let them know the subject needs to be revisited once tempers have calmed down and cooler heads prevail.

If someone is under the influence of drugs or alcohol, do not attempt to have a reasonable conversation with them. It is futile. They are not interested in coming to a resolution. They simply want to argue. At that point, they don't have the mental capacity to reason. They are led simply by the emotions of their deceitful heart. In their mind, they are right and that is all there is to it.

Listen to what James has to say:

"What causes fights and quarrels among you? Don't they come from your desires that battle within you? You desire but do not have, so you kill. You covet but you cannot get what you want, so you quarrel and fight. You do not have because you do not ask God" (James 4:1-3).

In other words, what is really upsetting you is that you can't have what you want. Because you can't have what you want, you lash out at others who can't give it to you. But you won't come to the source from which all blessings flow. This is really deep. It goes beyond a cry for attention or the need for sex, respect, or any kind of material possession. What is it that your heart and soul really longs for? The answer is simple: LOVE in its purest and most natural form.

Everything that the heart or soul could ever desire is wrapped up in love. Love protects, it covers, it builds up, it forgives, it heals, it casts out fear. It places no blame; it does not doubt. Love is total emotional security. When you are secure, you are at peace, and you won't have to fight to get it.

What James was trying to get us to see was that we are looking for love in all the wrong places. God is Love and EVERYTHING we need is in Him. All we have to do is simply ask and be willing to receive from Him. Unfortunately, everyone does not have this same revelation. So, because they don't get what they want, they feel they have to fight for it.

The battle is won in your mind. Reject toxic thoughts. Control your emotions. BREATHE. Listen to understand. Choose your words wisely. Respond in love. Learn to remain steady regardless of what is going on around you. Don't be moved by your emotions. You control your own narrative.

Choose the way of peace. Walking in love means considering the feelings of others before yourself and treating people right, regardless of how they treat you. Your words have power. They are seeds. What you say is what you will have. Speak highly of each other. Each one should hold the other in high esteem. Speak only positive things to and about one another. Never complain to friends or family about what is going on in your relationship. This can cause an even bigger divide in your home.

Don't be judgmental. Instead, show compassion. Restore them gently and cover them with love. Watch yourself so you do not get caught up in sin too. Watching someone fall or suffer because you knew you were right and they were wrong is NOT a win. When you are connected, especially in a covenant relationship like marriage, their loss is your loss.

In the heat of the moment, be sure to evaluate for danger and take appropriate action. Remove yourself and your children out of harm's way. If there are weapons in the house, know where they are at all times. It may help to have an alternate location to hide the weapon for personal safety of you and your loved ones. If they can't find the weapon, they can't use it on themselves or others. If you are in danger LEAVE, or hide and call 911.

This is for use in the unlikely event of an extreme emergency. Your safety and the safety of your family must come first. Take all threats of harm to self or to others seriously. If they start hinting or saying that they want to hurt themselves or someone else, it is time to take action, especially if they have the means to do it.

Never ignore the instinct that tells you when something is off with your loved one. It may be something they said, a change in their behavior, or just a feeling that you have inside that something is off. Go with your gut!

Don't be afraid to ask questions. Ask them how they are feeling and if they intend on doing themselves any harm. You can't be afraid to be direct. Their life, and possibly the lives of others, is at stake.

Be sure to check for threats like pills or weapons. Let them know that they are not alone and that you love and care for them. Keep them as calm as possible. Get help if there is immediate danger, call 911. Find a professional counselor or therapist if they don't already have one. If they do, check to see how soon you can get them in to be seen.

You can always call your local Suicide Prevention Hotline or the National Suicide Prevention Lifeline. Their phone number is (800) 273-8255. It is important to know the signs and to know what to do and when to spring into action. You must always remain vigilant.

There came a point where I became able to discern when it was him talking or when it was the alcohol talking. This helped me to know how to better deal with the situation. Him talking through the alcohol was a sign that there was a demonic spirit present. Again, this is not the scary Hollywood representation, but the enemy working through his mind to try to break us apart and destroy my faith.

Through Jesus, we have been given the power and authority over the enemy (Luke 10:19). The answer is simple: "Resist the devil and he will flee" (James 4:7). It says we are to submit to God by walking in the Spirit. When we do this, we stop focusing on what the enemy is trying to do, which is to provoke us to wrath. When you decide not to play with the enemy, he will take his ball and go home. He will leave you alone.

My go-to method was to set an atmosphere of worship in my home. When King Saul was troubled by an evil spirit, he sent for David to come play his harp for him. This would soothe and calm the king and the evil spirit would leave (1 Samuel 16:23).

I would turn on preaching or music and set my attention on the Lord. I refused to go back and forth with him in an argument when he was drunk. Eventually, he would drift off to sleep, or leave the room, or not engage at all. There were times that he would come in and be overcome with emotion because the music would touch his spirit and he would think about God's presence in his life.

Which leads me to an important point. Who am I to judge? You have no idea what a person has gone though in their past and how the Lord has brought them through. Their behavior and actions don't mean that they don't love the Lord or have some type of relationship with Him. Somewhere, they have been dropped and they are trying to find their way home through their pain. Just as Jesus did, we need to show compassion because their pain is not their fault.

Having said that, we STILL need to hold them accountable for their actions. Usually, the next day, after he would sober up, I could talk to him about what happened the night before. My husband loves his family. It's just that liquor gives him these Incredible Hulk moments and when he comes down, he realizes the damage that was done. Over the years, he has worked to improve this. I am proud of him for that. Some people are not willing to do the work. Although he still battles with the after effects of PTSD, he has found ways to better deal with himself and keep his emotions and behavior under control.

Abuse of any kind should never be tolerated. Never make excuses for it. Never blame yourself and never justify their actions because of their mental condition. That person must take accountability for their own actions. They must face the consequences for their behavior. Remember, you can never make someone take accountability until they are ready to do it for themselves and in their own time.

There are a lot of women that suffer in silence when they are in an abusive relationship. **Some women stay in abusive relationships because they don't know they are in one**. You know the saying, "What goes on in this house STAYS in this house." It's that kind of thinking and reasoning that keeps women in bondage when they are in abusive situations. There is a stigma attached to abuse. It is embarrassing and degrading, and nobody wants to look weak or helpless. So, we hide it, thinking we can handle it on our own. We put on a mask and pretend that everything is okay without seeking treatment or counseling. It only makes things worse.

Abuse comes in many forms: Physical, emotional, verbal, financial, and the list goes on. Don't think that because they don't put their hands on you that they are not abusive. Humiliation is another form of abuse where they may try to shame you or embarrass you in public. They may call you names, or are patronizing or dismissive.

They might be controlling, treating you like a child, spying on you or checking on your whereabouts. Control has to do with pride and fear. Pride is thinking that you are better than someone else. Fear is a tactic used to keep someone doing what you want them to do. Fear has to do with feeling out of control. GOD is in control. Submit to Him! In a healthy relationship there is no control, only respect and unity.

Emotional manipulation is where someone tries to gain power or control over someone else by using dishonest or manipulative tactics to get them to do what they want them to do. They may change up the facts or details, or twist your words to make it look like you were the one in the wrong. They may cause you to question or doubt yourself and make you feel like you are not good enough. They know your weakness and will use it against you. They are masters at mind games.

Most healthy relationships are based on mutual respect and trust. This means that we honor them for who they are without trying to change them or make them into someone that they are not, or do not wish to be. In return, we expect the same of them.

It is important to note that power is a part of all relationships. It just means that there is control (self-control), but this control is centered around the person being aware of their ability to influence their environment or the people around them.

When people control you, they don't respect you and they don't appreciate you. They certainly don't see any value in you. They want to change you or make you into the image that THEY want you to be. Perhaps, it is just to make you look bad so they can get some type of gain out of it, like promotion, recognition, authority, and influence.

Emotional manipulation can lead to serious issues like domestic violence and abuse. The person may become possessive and may want to control or dominate the other person. Whatever the situation, it is a form of emotional and mental abuse and can lead to many problems including stress, depression, and anxiety.

Financial abuse is where they control all the money, so if you did want to leave, you could not because you couldn't afford to do it. This is a big one for women. A lot of women stay in abusive situations because they cannot afford to get out. That is why it is so important for a woman to have her own money. Financial independence is of utmost importance and is also a form of self-care.

Paranoia is a symptom of PTSD. It creates trust issues and increases anxiety. Suspicion of infidelity and mistrust are an attack on the mind. It causes stress, intrusive thoughts and images, and leads to increased tension on the relationship. Hypervigilance sets in as the suspecting partner is waiting for the last shoe to drop, anticipating that something will happen. This can lead to destructive and abusive patterns of behavior.

Isolation of the spouse (even from friends and loved ones) is a tactic used to prevent cheating. In their mind, if they keep an eye on them and keep them away from being tempted, they can prevent the cheating. Threatening statements like "If you cheat on me, I'll kill you and them" are not empty threats. Do not take them lightly. It is a means to control your behavior with the consequences of your actions. This is abusive behavior whether they lay a hand on you or not.

In most cases, abuse does not happen out of nowhere. Most people don't notice right away. There are subtle hints that may slowly and eventually lead to more aggressive patterns of behavior. These small, subtle hints should trigger a red flag that something is not right with this person.

You have to be mindful about letting the little things slide because eventually, the little things can become big issues and cause more problems. People will try to use guilt and cause you to feel tricked or pressured into doing what they want you to do. They know how to spot your weakness and use it against you. This will keep happening until you make a decision to stop it.

You have to set boundaries. Boundaries will help you to clearly state your needs and outline what you are and are not willing to accept.

Simply put, abuse is the abnormal use of a person or a thing. Destructive behavior can be caused by past hurt. Unresolved anger can build and increase in intensity. Unforgiveness will hold your heart hostage and can manifest in the physical. In some cases, it is easier to get over being hurt physically than it is to get over being hurt mentally or emotionally. Hurt and frustration can lead to anger, which can lead to bitterness.

Some women are too embarrassed to ask for help. When you continue to suffer in silence you become desensitized and the abuse will become normal, almost a way of life. You come to expect it and accept it. This only gives the abuser permission to continue with their toxic behavior. You must decide for yourself when enough will be enough. If you have children, they are watching. They see this behavior. If you are not careful, they will take on the attitude of the abuser, or the one being abused. Their relationships will be patterned after your own, and they will live what they have seen.

The longer you are in the situation, the longer it will take to come out. When you are in a depressed state of mind, you have to put in the work to climb out of the hole you are in. By staying in that situation longer, you allow yourself to go deeper in that depression. Have you heard people talk about how they were in a "dark place"? This is where there is no joy to be found, no peace to be had. In this state, one can feel worthless and unlovable. They will lose interest in what used to excite them and struggle to believe that things will get better. So, they sink even further into this pit of despair. This is where thoughts of self-harm and suicide come from.

Once you have made the decision to make this type of change in your life you should have the right people to help you on your path. You need someone that has gone through it and that understands your struggles and can guide you on how to come out of this dark place. You need to connect with someone you trust that can show you how to let go of emotional toxins in order to live a happier, healthier, and more fulfilled life.

Don't suffer in silence any longer! Find some help. Ask a friend, join a support group. Seek counseling. Just begin your journey to healing. Find someone you can trust and let them know what's going on. Surround yourself with positive people that will encourage you. What you read and listen to is important as well. Cleanse your mind and your soul. You want to stop the patterns of toxic thinking and toxic behaviors in your life. Build yourself up starting with learning how to love YOU. Don't hide what you've been going through. Use it as a point of reference to show how far you have come, and then use it as an example to remind you of the things you will not accept anymore!

You are worth it! Your sanity is worth it. Your safety is worth it. Your future is worth it, as well. You are not alone, and you don't have to be. Someone is praying for you, and fighting, and waiting for you to reach out for help. But you must take the first step!!

Chapter 8: The Love Walk

Matthew 9:36 became the biggest help to me on my journey. It teaches me the correct perspective I should have as a PTSD Wife. It talks about Jesus traveling and healing the crowds of people that had flocked to him. It says, "When he saw the crowds, he felt compassion for them because they were distressed and dejected, like sheep without a shepherd."

The people were suffering and they had no help. Can you imagine what this must have felt like to them? What it must have done to their emotional wellbeing? It's one thing to be sick, but to not have any relief available and no help in sight, this must have caused major issues among themselves and their families. I'm sure they dealt with fear of the unknown, and people react differently when they are operating out of their own pain.

When Jesus came around, they saw Him as a representation of hope. I can imagine being one of Jesus's disciples always being surrounded and approached by sick people. It's not a place that I would want to be. Especially in this time of the pandemic that has taken over the world. But Jesus had a different way of looking at the situation. What He saw was that the people were sad, frustrated, mentally worn out, and in pain. These people needed His help.

From this, I learned to see my husband from a different point of view. First, I prayed and asked God to show me how to look at things through the eyes of Jesus. What I learned was that in order to see things through His eyes, I first needed to have His heart.

Love means different things to different people. Each definition comes from what they have experienced in their past. God is love and love comes through relationship. Sadly, the world has turned away from God and as a result, has turned away from love. Jesus knew this would happen. He said, "Then many will fall away, betray one another, and hate one another…because lawlessness will multiply, the love of many will grow cold" (Matthew 24:9-10, CSB).

The Bible is clear. God is Love. Love comes from Him. He loved us first and expects us to love each other. By showing love to others, we show our God in action to one another. Everything you need to know about love can be found in Jesus. He was our example here on earth about how we are to treat one another. He says in John 13:34-35, "I give you a new command: Love one another. Just as I have loved you, you are also to love one another. By this, everyone will know that you are my disciples, if you love one another" (CSB).

"Love is patient. Love is kind. Love does not envy, is not boastful, is not arrogant, is not rude, is not self-seeking, is not irritable, and does not keep record of wrongs. Love finds no joy in unrighteousness but rejoices in truth. It bears all things, believes all things, hopes all things, endures all things. Love never ends..." (1 Corinthians 13:4-8, CSB). Love is simply treating people as you should, not as they deserve. It is a constant decision. You must choose to walk in love, even when the situation does not warrant it.

When you feel loved and secure, you don't feel the need to attack someone. So, how do you get over hurt and frustration after being hurt in your relationship?

The answer is simple: Ask God to change you, heal you, and to restore the trust and intimacy in your marriage. Ask Him to show you what you need to see and what you need to change within yourself. Be sure to ask Him how to love your spouse and how to talk to them, and to show you what they need to feel loved and secure.

The enemy roams about like a roaring lion seeking whom he may devour. He comes when there is a fight. It is never a good idea to leave when you have had an argument. This is an opening for the enemy to come in and create division and cloud your mind and your judgement. This happened on *Grey's Anatomy*! Derrick and Addison were together and had a terrible fight and he went out to clear his mind and that's when he ran into Meredith Grey...and that was the end of Derrick and Addison. Don't give place to the devil. Your anger is a healthy, natural emotion. It is okay to validate the anger but be sure not to sin. In other words, manage your anger and keep the devil out of it.

Don't complain to others about your spouse. People will try to tell you what is best for you. "I wouldn't take that if I were you." You don't have to explain to anyone why you want your marriage to work. Fear of other people's opinion will disable you (Proverbs 29:25).

Every relationship deals with conflict. It's how you deal with that conflict that matters. You want to avoid conflict at all costs. But at some point, it's going to come up. When emotions begin to run high, try your best to defuse the situation. Proverbs 15:1 says, "A gentle answer turns away anger, but a harsh word stirs up wrath" (CSB).

Two wrongs never make a right. Never do the wrong thing to justify what they did to you. Your response should always be righteousness. This does not excuse abusive behavior. Redeem your spouse by treating them with love. Walk in love. Threats and rejection are not solutions. Fighting with fire only makes MORE fire. The key is to treat him like Jesus would treat him. Learn to see him through the eyes of the Lord. As the wife, you have the POWER to change your husband's heart by the way you treat him. If you want him to act better, you should start by treating him better.

Let your words be seasoned with grace and love. Hurtful words and actions break trust and cause problems with intimacy. Use your words to build them up, to heal them, and to love them. Don't used your words to destroy. Think before you speak. There may be consequences for what you say. You cannot take it back once it has been released into the atmosphere. The Bible says we should be "Quick to listen, slow to speak, and slow to anger" (James 1:19). Practice active listening. Wait for your turn to talk rather than listening to make your point. Listen to what the other is saying and work together to come to a solution or some sort of agreement.

It also helps to learn how your spouse communicates. If two people communicate in two different ways, the message will get lost. Your point of view is based on your personal, past experience and knowledge. Communication is made up of what you say (words), how you say it (tone), and the spirit in which you say it (attitude). The right combination of these three components will deliver the right message the right way and at the right time. Timing is everything. Look for the healthy way to communicate what you are feeling. Take time to breathe and construct your sentence in such a way that will clearly communicate your intentions while considering the other person.

Tell the truth in love. Express how you feel, but make sure that love is the foundation. You can lose your message in the way that it is communicated. When you criticize, it turns the blame on them. Phrases like "You always…" or "You never…" only add fuel to the fire. When you complain, it shifts the conversation around you, how your feel, and your experience. "When you did this, it made me feel like…"

Gentleness is love in action. It is also a Fruit of the Spirit, which is evidence that the Spirit is at work in us. To be gentle is not a sign of weakness. It is easy to go off on someone, especially when they are treating you bad, but self-restraint takes much work and discipline. Do not allow yourself to be controlled by your emotions.

Be persistent in being gentle. It may fix your problem. It can lead them to be more open to turn from their anger, work toward fixing the issue, and to try to understand where you are coming from. Gentleness breaks down a person's defense. I can't receive a message if it is delivered in a rude or toxic manner. Maturity is revealed in how you talk to people. When trying to get your point across, remember that if you are pleasant, you will be more persuasive to people. You get more bees with honey.

God has drawn us with loving kindness. We should draw others with this same kind of love. Gentleness is connected to kindness. If you want respect, you have to give respect, no matter how they treat you. Walking in love is a constant decision. The phrase "Nice girls never win" is a lie. Proverbs 11:16 says that a woman of gentle grace will be respected. You don't have to be rude to get your point across.

Gentleness defuses conflict. It takes TWO fools to fight. If you "match their energy" it will not help. It only makes matters worse and will add to the tension. When you don't clap back, you silence the haters because you don't give them anything to go off. It's okay to disagree. It doesn't mean that anyone is more right or wrong than the other. Just agree to respectfully disagree. The keyword here is RESPECT. Find out how to come to a conclusion that is mutually beneficial. Is it more important to get your point across? Or to keep your relationship?

Get to the root and focus on the actual issue at hand in that moment. Where did this behavior come from? Call it out. Identify it. Who did it to you? Is there trauma at the root? This is the area to pinpoint for prayer.

Give grace for mistakes. Try not to be easily offended. Offense can lead to a cold heart. There is no love, no compassion. A heart of stone is what the enemy wants; showing no grace or mercy to one another. This causes division and separation. You must protect your heart and continue to work on keeping yourself free from that which binds you. Accept your anger, but don't internalize it. Release it and let it go.

We are God's ambassadors here on earth. We are His representation for those that don't believe. You judge when you don't show grace. Saying things like "That's what you get" is you passing judgement on others. Can you, or will you still love them even if they don't agree with you? When you judge, the words you throw can be hard as stones. We have been saved by grace for good works. Sometimes, we treat people according to their story, by who they are right now, and not who they are called to be.

You are no better than your spouse. You both need grace. Shame, condemnation, and guilt are all connected. Grace is a lifeline. Stop holding their failures and shortcomings against them. It is by grace that we ALL have been saved.

So, how do you walk in love with someone that has hurt you? Forgiveness is the key! Forgiveness is not just saying "It's okay" when someone apologizes. It's not excusing the words and actions of someone that has caused you pain. It is an actual process of letting go of both the offense and the offender. You will free yourself of the internal toxins, mental weights, and physical illness that comes with emotional baggage. Emotional baggage is unprocessed, negative feelings that have built up from past negative experiences.

Forgiveness is not about you being weak and letting someone get away with walking all over you or taking advantage of you. In fact, forgiveness is about you having the power and taking control of your life. Forgiveness will keep you free. Being able to control your emotions will reduce the stress and anxiety that comes with toxic relationships or situations.

Forgiveness protects your mind. Your mind controls your body, but YOU can control your mind. Everything starts with a thought! Forgiveness is a decision that has to be made over and over again. After an offense, you may resolve your issue with the person, but later, when the feelings come back, or if your memory is triggered, you will be back in the same mind space. You must make the decision to release the offense and the offender every time the thought comes to your mind.

Empathy is looking at the situation from the other person's point of view. Some things to consider would be what is going on with that person to make them act that way? Were they under pressure? Consider their past. What life experiences made them that way? And how might they be seeing the situation different than you are? What was your role in the situation? Could you have said or done anything that may have provoked them? What were their overall intentions? Were they trying to help or give constructive criticism? It may have gotten lost in translation or in their behavior. You may learn a lot about someone by just taking a moment to consider their point of view. It can change the whole conversation. Mutual respect is the common goal.

Not forgiving someone does NOT protect you from not being hurt again in the future. In fact, there is no guarantee that the person will apologize to you. That is why you have to learn to release toxic thoughts and toxic people from your life.

Taking accountability is more than just admitting guilt and saying you're sorry. When you are accountable, you take ownership over your words and actions, and you take responsibility for the ripple effect they caused. It is not about placing blame on someone else. "I did this only because you said, or you did..." You are in charge of your own behavior. The things you do and say (for the most part) are your choice.

Whatever you say was on your mind. It's the same thing with your actions. If you did it, it was on your mind to do. If your intention is to hurt someone and you act on it, you must take accountability for that action. To make the situation right, you must admit to it, take full responsibility, and do what you can to make amends for what you have done.

To repent means to turn away from a negative behavior in order to get back on track and headed in the right direction. In the Bible, repentance is accompanied by forgiveness and a restoration of what should have been, or a promise of better things to come.

"If my people who are called by my name humble themselves and pray and seek my face and turn from their wicked ways, then will I hear from heaven and will forgive their sin and heal their land" (2 Chronicles 7:14).

The takeaway from that is when you ask for forgiveness it should be granted. But know that offenses block blessings from getting to you. When you take accountability and ask for forgiveness and change your ways, forgiveness can be granted, and your mistakes will not be able to keep you from what should be rightfully yours.

Chapter 9: It Starts with a Thought

I am a person that wears their heart on their sleeve. You will always know what I am feeling because it will always show on my face, or through my words and actions. It seems I always find the worst times to cry. I tell myself, "You better not cry. Don't cry. Suck it up." But that never works. I find that this only makes me cry even more. I cry at everything. When I am happy. When I am sad. When I am angry. I even cry watching commercials.

To start things off, let me first say, there is nothing wrong with feeling your emotions and letting them out. The problem comes when we act on the emotions and make decisions and judgements based on them. This can get us in a world of trouble.

Emotions are controlled by your thoughts. Everything we do in life starts with a thought. It is our job to process those thoughts, to accept or reject them. It's all up to you. You control your emotions by controlling the way you think. We can change our lives by simply changing the way we think. It is the mind that controls the body. Bad thinking will lead to bad behavior. To make lasting change in your life, you must stop making decisions and assumptions based on how you feel. How you feel is temporary. Your feelings will lie and take you down the wrong path. Don't follow your heart. Remember, the heart is deceitful.

So, who is controlling you? Whatever is at work on the inside will show up on the outside through your words and actions. There is a constant internal fight for control happening, even right now as you read this. It's like on the old TV shows where the person has a little angel on one shoulder and a little devil on the other. Both are whispering trying to persuade the character to do things their way. This is real life! The Spirit of God within you is at constant war with your flesh (Galatians 5:17). It's up to you to decide who will take the wheel and govern your mind.

Negative, hurtful words said to you plant a seed. Think of it as a curse. There's an old saying: Whatever you water will grow. So, you have to make the decision. Will you water the blessing? Or will you water the curse? Learn to reject the curse. Protect your mind!! We must take every thought captive...hold that thought!! And then filter it through the process of elimination. Examine your thoughts to find out which builds you up and which tears you down. Then, remove the bad. Take out what goes against what you know to be true.

Side Note: The reason that some bad or negative thoughts resonate with you is because to some degree there is some truth to them. However, the trick is, you have to be able to break down that thought so you can get to the root of it to find out what you need to work on. As the old saying goes, chew the meat and spit out the bone.

Self-control is a Fruit of the Spirit. It takes time to develop. It is living by the Spirit. "Walk in the Spirit and you will not fulfill the lust of the flesh" (Galatians 5:16). "Submit yourself to God, resist the devil and he will flee" (James 4:7).

The Spirit brings inner peace and stability. Your flesh, or your natural instinct, wants to do what feels good. Train yourself to be controlled. Replace negative thinking, words, and actions with the opposite. Read, study, and pray daily. Your desire will change. Discipline yourself by denying what your flesh tells you. You have the power.

Fear will paralyze you. It is connected to stagnation. There is no movement, no growth, and no progress or development. Fear will keep you from trying. Low self-esteem and insecurity are all deeply rooted in fear and will project on to your spouse while keeping you both bound.

So how do you combat fear?? You do that with self-love and assurance. This will help to build your confidence. It starts with understanding who you are as a person. Knowing what you bring to the table, what you are capable of, who you are called to serve, and how you are called to serve them. Your assignment is to serve your spouse, just as their assignment is to serve you.

Be willing to learn from your mistakes and grow from them. They are not the end of the road, but new opportunities for you to reflect the Love of God while growing together in love and strengthening your bond.

Address your fears head on and get to the root of what is causing them. Share them with your spouse and work together to come to resolution. This will determine the direction you need to take. Break it down and simplify it. This will bring clarity and direction.

Negative emotions like fear, anxiety, and shame are all tools of the enemy. As I started my journey to renew my mind, the very first verse I memorized was 2 Corinthians 10:5. It teaches us that we are to take hold to every thought and make it obedient to Christ. How do we do this? Hold it up to the Word of God and get rid of anything that is not of Him, His way, or His will.

Take a moment to think. How is your storm manifesting in your life? What affect does it have? Sometimes it may be hard to pinpoint exactly what you are feeling. When you are in distress there are so many mixed emotions that can be at work in you. Self-awareness will help you identify what you are feeling. Be real with yourself. What are you feeling? Why are you feeling it? What can you do about it? Are these emotions helping you in this moment?

Learn how to challenge your emotions. Use them for self-improvement to help you change or get rid of the things that no longer serve you at this place in your life and in your relationship. Use those emotions to help others. Refuse to be offended and don't take things so personal. Could it be that your spouse is reacting out of their own pain? They may not be able to express what it is they are going through. Or they may not be able to control their outburst. Their behavior does not speak to who you are. Maturity is displayed by how you treat people despite how they treat you. It's all about your response. Consider the source and look past their behavior to see their pain and the possible cause of their behavior.

Unresolved anger can lead to health problems, both physical and mental. Holding it all in can eat away at you on the inside. Depression related to trauma is a result of holding on to the pain of your past. Retaliation can cost you, especially if your anger becomes uncontrollable.

Your mind will reflect what is in your heart, and what is in your heart will come out of your mouth when you are under enough pressure. The enemy will magnify situations to distract you. It may help to change your environment. I know you will not always be able to change your actual location, but you can change the environment right where you are. Set the mood for what you want to feel. Change the sound. You can play music, read scriptures aloud, listen to preaching, affirmations, or anything that feeds your soul.

Emotions are clues to what still needs your attention in your life, and they let you know what you still need to work on. These are the issues you cannot fix on your own. You need the Lord to help you. There are times when one can become bitter or resentful because of their experience dealing with PTSD as a spouse. It feels unfair and unwarranted. Because of what they are going through, we choose not to address the issues we may be having with them for fear that it may seem insensitive to their needs. It may cause them to have an episode. When the time is right, have the important conversations to express what is bothering you in a way that respects them while letting them know how their actions are affecting you and your household.

There is an agenda behind negative thoughts. It is to distract you from what they are really doing to you in a place that you don't realize. Other areas of your life are affected socially, mentally, and physically. Once you figure out where else you are being affected, you can target these areas and work on improving them. Everything we do in life starts with a thought. It is our job to process those thoughts and then decide whether to accept or reject them. It's all up to you. Words are seeds. This is why it is important to filter your thoughts. Whatever you say will be and what you allow in your mind is what you will say.

2 Corinthians 10:5 tells us we need to demolish arguments and every proud (high) thing that is raised up against the knowledge of God, and we take every thought captive to obey Christ. Words said in the heat of the moment can hurt. They can pierce your heart and can sink in, causing emotional damage. When emotional outbursts are fueled by drugs or alcohol, it is difficult for the mind to know when to stop the lips from moving. The point of the argument at that point is to win at all costs, and the strategy will be to say what will hurt you the most and shut you down. Don't be drawn in by this. The book of Proverbs is full of advice on how to avoid being drawn into arguments.

In order to be effective, letting go of the pain and hurt of the past will require a combination of healthy habits and a positive mindset. You have to change the way you think in order to change the way you behave or react to certain situations.

Holding on to the pain of the offense can create more damage than what was originally done. By letting go of grudges and bitterness you can improve your health and gain peace of mind. Forgiveness can lead to healthier relationships, improved mental health, less anxiety, stress, and hostility, better physical health, a stronger immune system, improved self-esteem, and it can reduce symptoms of depression.

Be mindful of your inner dialog; the conversations you have with yourself. Acknowledge your emotions and work through them. Move away from your role as a victim in order to find your power, and release the control that the person had over your life. As you move away from grudges, you will no longer define your life by how you have been hurt.

Learn to replace hostility and bitterness with peace. You cannot continue to punish your loved one by holding on to grudges and acting cold or distant towards them. This can do more harm than what was done by the original offense. You have to find a way to replace your resentment with what will bring peace to the situation. Learn to avoid triggers and separate yourself from negative emotions.

Boundaries are created first and foremost to protect you from harm. By establishing boundaries, you will teach people how to treat you and clearly define your expectations for the relationship.

Limit your interaction with people that try to manipulate you. Try to increase the physical distance between them and you. If you have to be around them, don't allow their words to draw you in. They may pick a fight or try to get you out of character. That is another form of manipulation. Don't give them that much power over you.

The boundaries you have set should have consequences. Once they cross the line, especially if they continue to violate your boundary, you may have to stop all contact with them until their behavior changes. They may realize their wrong and correct it immediately or they may not. A person can change, but they must be willing to do so.

You aren't responsible for anyone's behavior but your own. Putting boundaries in place will help you to improve your mental wellbeing, become more self-aware, help to reduce your stress levels, and improve overall health.

Chapter 10: Family Matters

Family is important! Believe it or not, it is the family that has the biggest impact and influence on society. People come from different walks of life, different backgrounds, values, and beliefs. Every person has their own unique experience in life, and this is what drives a person to think and act a certain way. The way we are as individuals can be traced back to the lessons we learned during our upbringing and early development in childhood. This is how we navigate through the world and relate to others.

Family is a foundational relationship. As a child, you learn how to relate to the world by what you have experienced right there in your household. If you ever wonder why someone is the way they are, check their history. The family, along with their personal journey as a member of that family, shapes and develops the individual into who they will be, what they believe, and what they value.

God's ultimate goal is for us to be reconciled with Him and with one another. The goal of the enemy is to destroy the family. Family is the basic unit of society. In fact, it is the foundation of society. A healthy family will produce productive members of the community. But a house divided will not be able to stand (Mark 5:25). If the house falls, society falls too.

You can look at what is going on in the world today and see what is going on in the family. If you look at men and women that have been imprisoned, people with mental illness or behavior issues (not related to a chemical imbalance), or even a child in foster care or a juvenile facility, the majority of them have experienced some external stress factors that go back to their childhood. It can be any of three categories: Neglect—where the child was left alone to fend for themselves. Abuse—whether verbal, physical, emotional, or sexual. Or tragedy involving a near-death experience or the death of a loved one, like a parent or close friend or relative.

The effects of trauma are far reaching. It creates a ripple effect that extends beyond that moment, that day, and even the person that it happened to. PTSD affects the whole house, including the children. What they see can affect them. Living in a toxic environment and witnessing the after effects of trauma in the home can cause irreparable damage if you are not careful to guard against it.

Trauma can be passed down. Even though they were not the

ones that experienced it, a child can be limited by the fears and negative thinking of their parent. Hurt people hurt people. It's not always intentional. It may be them acting out of their fear or regret. They can put too much pressure on the child. Someone that has been violated may have a hard time connecting with others and may not be in a position to be able to show love and affection to their child. A cold or distant parent will create a cold and distant child. It affects the individual person. They may become withdrawn or angry, aggressive, or verbally abusive. This can affect their relationships. It's not just their marriage. Their parenting can become affected. This is why having a strong, healthy family unit is so important.

As a PTSD Wife, sometimes you will have to fill in the gap and be the mediator between your spouse and your children or loved ones. A breakdown in communication can lead to a divide in certain relationships. Try your best to keep the peace in the house. A lot of times, those that are closest receive the wrong end of misguided emotions and mental anguish. PTSD does not cause the problem, but it can put a strain on your important relationships.

As a result of pain that has been passed down, children can experience anxiety or depression and begin displaying undesirable behavior or acting out at school, at home, and in other social settings. Unresolved anger can lead to bitterness. The child may become upset with the parent that is acting out, or the one that is allowing it to happen. Older children may become upset about having to take on the role of caretaker, becoming the adult in the situation. They may grow to resent the parent (or both parents) for having to miss out on "normal" life because all of the focus in the house is on the parent with the issue.

As a parent, our responsibility is to set the pattern for our children. To protect them and teach them what is right. To be the example of the type of person we want them to be. There has been a falling away from God and His ways, and the world is hurting from it. Today, we are losing the leadership and guidance of parents. If we lose the parents, then we lose the kids because they have nobody to guide them in the way that they should go. Because of this, children are being left unprotected and exposed to too many things before their time.

Kids these days are having ADULT problems! Teen pregnancy, addiction, homicidal tendency, suicidal thoughts, depression, and anxiety. Did you know that the rate of depression in military kids is actually higher than other teens because of the stress that comes with military life? They are vulnerable, and they are the ones that are suffering because of the actions (or non-actions) of the parents. This is where it becomes a problem for our society.

When these kinds of issues are left untreated, it keeps them from being able to function in the home, or at school, and in the community. And when they are not able to function in society, it can lead to trouble, poverty, crime, homelessness, and incarceration.

It is time to bring the family back together. Encourage them to be more effective by becoming more active and involved in parenting, strengthening relationships, and sharpening the necessary tools needed for family success. A successful family will produce children that will become productive, engaged citizens that contribute to building up our communities and not tearing them down.

Just like anything in nature, the right atmosphere is conducive to positive growth. What you surround them with is what will develop. The key is to surround them with what builds them up. Your words of affirmation and love will imbed a sense of pride and strengthen their self-esteem. Love is a tool. Your words are seeds. What you water is what will grow.

Your words create the atmosphere of your home. They all matter, the ones you speak, and even the ones you do not speak. Proverbs 14:1 says that a wise woman builds her house and a foolish one tears it down. How is this done? Through your words!

Your words have the power to shape the world around you. They can bring life or death. Speak what you want to be. Call it into existence. When you do this, you are activating your faith. You are believing God for what is to come, even if it doesn't look like it right now.

What you say is governed by what you feel in your heart. That is why it is important to guard your heart. While you cannot protect your heart from experiencing pain, you can guard it from holding on to hurt, which can lead to bitterness. By letting go of offense, disappointment, and regret of the past, you will keep your heart free, which will keep you from speaking negativity into existence. Put your faith into practice and speak life over everything: Your marriage, your family, and yourself.

It starts with the foundation. You cannot build a house on sand and expect it to stand. As soon as a storm comes, it will wash the house away. There's an old hymn that says, "On Christ the solid rock

I stand, all other ground is sinking sand." Your home needs a solid foundation to stand on, and that is the Lord.

When I was growing up, church was not an option. If you were in the house, and you were a child (no matter how old you were), you were going to be in the House of the Lord on Sunday morning. I can remember spending Saturday night hanging out late with my friends. No matter what time I came in and went to bed, I had better be ready on time for service in the morning. Yes, church was a place that I learned more about the Bible, God, and His son Jesus. But for me, church became the center of my social life. The church was more than just some old stuffy place that I dreaded going to each Sunday morning. It was my world.

Church is a filling station. We go there to get what we need so that we can go out in the world and pour out God's Love in places of darkness and despair. Being in the atmosphere and around likeminded people helped to shape my view of the world and of myself. It allowed me the opportunity to grow in my faith, be active in community, and increase in knowledge of who I am and who I was called to be. It was a cocoon that provided protection and cultivated my transformation into young adulthood.

My church was the local hotspot for young people. All the cool kids were there. Of course, we had Sunday School, the youth choir, and the junior usher board. There were lock-ins, youth retreats, field trips, and more. We even had a basketball and cheer team, as well as a performance drill team. Each year, the church would go to the convention and participate in the national orator's competition (of which I once won first place).

The main goal of the church, outside of increasing your faith, is for spiritual development and self-improvement. It helps to develop a moral compass, the tiny voice inside that governs their decisions as they navigate the world around them. The church provides a sense of community. We are all brothers and sisters working together toward the same goal. Sunday School helps children to learn and understand the Word and cultivate a relationship with God at their own level. It is through the church that we find identity and purpose. Everything you need is in the church. The people that make up the church are so diverse, having different talents and skillsets. The church is self-sufficient.

Regularly attending church as a family promotes unity and family bonding. It is linked to a decrease in domestic abuse, suicide, teen pregnancy, and divorce. What you learn in church can also hea marriages and restore relationships. As a wife and mother, you are the anchor of the family and you set the tone of the house. There needs to be some sense of stability, discipline, and consistency in the home. Being active in your local church will provide this for you. I made a choice that as for me and my house, we will serve the Lord, and not once have I regretted it.

Unfortunately, PTSD can create a divide in the home. It is important that you stand on your faith to navigate through these tough times. Don't become so overwhelmed and distracted by what is going on with your spouse that you neglect the rest of your family and yourself, especially your children. Problems in the home can lead to problems at school and in their social life. Look for patterns of unhealthy behaviors that have been passed down through growing up in a toxic environment.

If you want to change the generations, you must talk to your kids. Tell them the truth. No more family secrets. Stop hiding things and covering up dysfunction. Speak to them on their level so they will understand. Let them know what runs in their family, what generational spirits they will have to fight, what traps they need to watch out for, what strongholds run through their bloodline, and what they need to protect themselves against. Tell them their history and the challenges those before them had to face. Most of all… TELL THEM WHAT GOD HAS DONE! How He made a way, how He brought (and BOUGHT) them out, and how He changed the whole story. Give them your God.

Children see what is going on. They can harbor unhealthy emotions based on what is happening in their family life. Check their social connections. Make sure they are in healthy relationships and hanging with the right kind of crowd. Preventive care is best. Take the steps to keep them covered. Spend time with them to let them know they matter. Family game nights, family outings, movie time, and more are great ways to do this.

Nothing brings a family together like a meal made with love! The Dinner Table is a sacred space where families come together to create memories and bond over food and fellowship. It is a place of Love, Healing, Support and Encouragement. It builds Confidence, Self-Awareness, and Interpersonal Skills. It promotes Unity, Peaceful Resolution, and a Sense of Pride. If you want to heal the World, heal the Family. If you want to heal the Family, it starts at the Dinner Table.

Spend time with your children. Talk to them. Not just to fuss but find out about their day. What they're up to. Find out their dreams and their plans. Support them in it. Quality time is a must! Create some traditions for your family. For us, it's Christmas and vacations, both of which started with my dad and his family. Christmas is serious business around our house. We go all the way out! It's the same with family vacations. We're going to fuss through the whole thing and get on each other's nerves (I like to say that's part of the magic), but we wouldn't trade it for the world. The memories you create with your family are PRICELESS! And what they learn from you, they will pass down to their families.

Don't wait until you are able to do the big things. It's the everyday things that matter. Movie night. Family game night. Go bowling. Take a walk around your neighborhood. Find things to do in your community.

Parents have to be more involved. The amazing wife and mother depicted in Proverbs 31 is described as knowing the affairs of her house (verse 27). She is aware of what is going on because she is present and observant. She stays ready to spring into action. That same verse says she does not eat the bread of idleness. That means when she observes that something is wrong, or off, she corrects it right away instead of letting it continue to build and destroy her household.

This is how we must be as women. Monitor what is coming in and what's going on in the house. The way technology is set up these days, there should be less concern about what your child has access to, and more concern about what has access to your child. Remain vigilant. Meet your children's friends. Don't be afraid to ask questions. Where are you going? Who are you going with? Who's going to be there? What are y'all doing there? Will there be drinking? Drugs? Don't be afraid to ask! Follow your gut. Instinct and intuition are God's gifts to women. Don't ignore that feeling when something seems off. That thought you have that something isn't right. Search their rooms, flip the mattress. Check the drawers. I don't believe in closed doors in my house unless you are changing clothes or in the bathroom. Investigate and make no apology. They will thank you for it later.

Chapter 11: The Reset

Your mental health matters too. Take heed to yourself. Negative thoughts, emotional stress, and feeling overwhelmed are all signs that you need a reset. Being tired emotionally means that you are worn down spiritually. Remember, you are blessed even when you are at the end of your rope (Matthew 5:3). There is help. Don't lose hope. "Come to me, all who are weary and burdened, and I will give you rest" (Matthew 11:28). Make time to reset, refresh, and refill your spirit. As you walk in unity and pour out love on your husband, allow God to pour His love into you.

Love is a basic human need. It is a tool. We use it to heal, to cover, to protect, and so much more. Because we were created for connection, we show our love to people through the things we say and do. The Bible teaches that we are to put our interests behind the interests of others. We are to consider our neighbor first, and wherever there is a need, we are to fulfill it. "Love fulfills the law" (Romans 13:10).

Yes, God wanted us to show our love and serve one another, but He never intended for us to give so much to the point where there is nothing left for ourselves. In the scripture, there are a few stories where Jesus has drawn away from the crowd in order to take a break and rest from all the work He was doing. If you don't allow yourself the time needed to refresh and refuel, you will find yourself drained, which can affect your physical, emotional, and spiritual health.

You are responsible for your own happiness. It is not found in the validation or opinion of others. Happiness is choosing what to accept in your life and knowing what and when to let go. It is finding peace in the decisions you make and having the courage to stick with it. You should have confidence in who you are and be bold enough not to make excuses or apologize for being authentically you. You must find the strength to move forward when everything around you seems to be falling apart.

Tending to the needs of your spouse as a PTSD Wife can take away from other areas of your life. Your health, your children, your career, and other aspects of your life can suffer without having the proper amount of care and attention to them. You must find balance.

Did you know that 22% of family caregivers have reported that their own health has declined since they began caring for their loved one? The emotional and physical stress of the job can take a toll on their wellbeing. As a PTSD Wife, you are a caregiver, having to drop everything to care for your spouse while they are in need. "Greater love has no man than this: That someone lay down his life for a friend" (John 15:13).

Take care of your temple. Healing your body starts on the inside with tending to your emotional wellbeing. Be mindful about what your body is saying to you. Stress, depression, anxiety, and grief can cause physical problems in your body, and can affect your relationship with the people that have to be around you. Slow down. Be kind to yourself. Take heed to your mind, body, and soul. They are all connected.

Pay close attention to your emotions and the things that cause you to "act out of character." Those are the tell-tale signs that there is a deeper issue you have yet to work through, a past pain to process, or an emotional challenge you have yet to overcome. The truth is, if it still hurts then you are not over it yet. Let these moments be a guide to help you pinpoint areas of your life to improve on.

You are what you eat. Not just the food on your plate, but everything you take in. Everything you watch. Everything you hear. Everything you allow to penetrate your soul. Take control of your emotional wellbeing. Become more aware of who and what you allow to have access to you. Reject negative thinking and toxic attitudes. Fight fear with faith and action, and surround yourself with Love, Light, and Positive Energy. A healthy mind, much like a healthy body, requires balance and nutrition, determination and consistency, and a desire for change and overall improvement. Through your healing, you will become better equipped to face the challenges of the world around you.

Protect your peace. Set boundaries and enforce them. You are not a doormat, a punching bag, nor a trash can. You deserve to be loved with dignity, honor, and respect. The fact that they know you won't leave them is not a license to abuse or mistreat you with their hands, their words, or anything else. Love is an ACTION. Words are not enough. Your emotional wellness depends on a healthy environment.

Be sure to set boundaries and learn how to harness the power of "NO." Self-care is the highest form of love you can give yourself, and you are worth it. Boundaries are important because they set the guidelines of how you want to be treated. It ensures that your relationship is mutually respectful, supportive, and caring. Boundaries also protect you from being exploited. They help you avoid getting too close to people who don't have your best interests at heart.

When someone knows they have crossed a boundary with you, they are less likely to repeat the offense. However, the ones that continually disrespect the boundary you have put in place should not be allowed to take up space in your life anymore. This is called protecting your peace.

Emotional Self-Care is about being aware of what you are feeling and taking the time to work through those emotions in a healthy way. I have found that one of the best ways to do this is through journaling. To begin with, it helps to reduce stress and anxiety because essentially, you are doing a data dump from your head onto the paper. It helps to uncover what is really bothering you. If you write about what's bothering you or what's making you feel a certain way, it helps to calm your nerves and also gives you the opportunity to brainstorm for the solutions to your problems.

Journaling also helps to relieve symptoms of depression and can aid in the healing process after a traumatic event. It also helps you to discover your voice, which is key in setting boundaries.

Find something that gives you joy, makes you smile, or relaxes you and COMMIT to doing that thing for 15-30 minutes each day. Whether it's taking a walk, reading, or watching your favorite sitcom. Diet, exercise, rest, and find ways to reduce stress. Don't miss your scheduled routine checkups with your doctor. Preventive care is best. Don't wait until there is an issue.

Do you get enough sleep? If the answer is NO, then you are not alone. Studies show that 70% of caregivers suffer from a lack of sleep. Burning the candle at both ends is not productive and it can be harmful to your health. My husband struggles with sleep and often wakes me up. When he is up in the middle of the night, I am awake with him. Sometimes I find it hard to get back to sleep. I wake up in the morning feeling like I got no rest at all. This may cause me to feel drained throughout my day. I may experience headaches and not be able to concentrate like I need to. Make time for you to regenerate, reenergize, and refresh yourself mentally and physically.

Seek both professional and spiritual help for your issues. Speak to a counselor or coach to help you work through any issues or to achieve personal wellness goals. Your emotions are tied to what is in your heart. When you heal your heart, you heal your mind. When you heal your mind, you change your behavior. When you change your behavior, you change your relationships.

Remember, PTSD only highlights the issues in your marriage. Your spouse is not necessarily the problem! They are a mirror reflecting YOUR ability to Love unconditionally, to Forgive continually, and to Overcome obstacles in your relationship. Resist feelings of Resentment toward them. CHANGE YOUR FOCUS and see the challenge as way to improve YOURSELF for the situation.

What is the situation teaching you about yourself? What do you need to change? What do you need to improve? What do you need to stop? What do you need to do more of? What skill/tool do you need to help you through this moment? What does your spouse need from you in this situation? Are you able to provide it? Are you willing to provide it? Why or why not? Are you okay with them turning to someone else to meet this need? What does the Word say? Ask the Experts. Google scriptures/inspirational quotes. "What does the Bible say about _____." Write them down. Memorize them— make it stick. **Constant review is the student's glue!** Apply them— it won't work unless you work it!

Find your tribe. There is strength in numbers. You cannot and should not do this alone. Connect with others who have the same goal in mind as you. It is good to find someone that is going through or has gone through the same things you are experiencing. Community only makes us stronger. Draw from their strength and learn from their weakness as you grow. Support and lean on each other as you go.

When you are going through problems in your marriage due to PTSD, you may feel the need to distance yourself from friends and family. Sometimes it can be because you are ashamed of what is going on in the house. You may fear being judged by people that don't understand. Sometimes their behavior can be unpredictable, and it may be easier to just not invite anyone over to your house.

If you are going through your own personal depression, you may want to be left alone. The depression can be brought on because you are fighting feelings of loneliness and feel like you have no one that cares about you. This can put a strain on the relationships you do have because you will have a distorted view of reality. But if over time you continually reject the hand that people extend to you, they will stop offering it. Therefore, it is important not to isolate yourself. Community will help to combat depression brought on by isolation. We were created for connection and interaction with each other.

Put systems in place that will help to lighten the load: Babysitters, food delivery services, afterschool sports/enrichment programs, and friends and family that can step in when needed. Giving yourself a break takes the pressure off of you to perform beyond your limit. Wives and moms are often pulled in many directions, and it can be overwhelming. You can be every woman and can do all things, but you just can't do it all at one time. Pace yourself. Delegate some responsibilities to family members.

Feeling overwhelmed is a sign that some area of your life is out of balance. Here's some practical tips that may help:

Hebrews 12:1 - Let go of the people, places, and things that weigh you down.

Ephesians 5:15-17 - Prepare and plan ahead to make the best use of your time.

Mark 6:30-31 - Make time for YOU. Don't be so consumed that you neglect yourself.

Philippians 4:8 - Protect your peace by choosing what you want to focus on.

Believe it or not, having a clean house can ease tension in the relationship. It has been said that a cluttered space, like your home or your car, can reveal a cluttered mind. Make it a habit to clean and purge what is not needed. When your space is cluttered and out of order, it is a sign that something in your life is out of balance. It could be your time management, your workload, or simply your priorities. It proves that your energy and attention is focused elsewhere. This can actually show up in your relationship.

Have you ever seen the show *Hoarders*? It's about people who live in homes that are filled with an unhealthy level of clutter. In most cases, there is an emotional connection with this type of behavior. The clutter is a result of what happens when people do not address their issues. They may not want to let go of certain items because they hold cherished memories, an emotional connection, or a sense of security. It may also be a lack of zest for life. They may have all but given up in their mind. These conditions usually affect their relationships with those that love them. Cleaning the clutter forces them to address those issues and make changes.

Some may view a dirty house as a sign that the person just does not care enough about themselves or the people they live with. Some may find that one person is waiting on the other to do the work, thinking it is not their job. This adds more pressure to an already hectic schedule and can make things worse.

The bottom line is that a clean house will make one less thing there is to fight about. Everyone should be a part of keeping the house neat and in order, picking up after themselves. Teach children how to do this at their own level. Divide your house into four main areas and create a schedule to clean each area on a regular basis. This way, you won't be overwhelmed by having to do it all in one day. A little bit at a time, spaced out through the week will allow you more time to focus on the other tasks and matters at hand that need to be addressed.

Schedule your day accordingly and prioritize your time. Decide what is most important and plan your day around it. Set deadlines and checkpoints to help manage your time. This will require planning ahead. If you have control of your house, it will help to keep tension down and avoid unnecessary stress.

Get wise with your money. Financial struggles are one of the leading causes of marital discord. Learn to budget, shop wisely, and save up for a rainy day. Tap into your own skills, gifting, and talents to discover untapped possible sources of income. When you can help ease the financial burden of the house, you will take the pressure off your spouse. This can help to reduce the frequency of arguments and promote a peaceful environment.

Financial security and stability are all a part of self-care. It's time to put your business affairs in order! A woman should have income of her own and she should also be aware of the location and content of important documents like:

- Insurance Policies (including her own)

  - Includes Life, Home, Car, etc.

- Wills

- Birth/death certificates

- DD214s

- Bank account info

- Social Security cards

- Marriage certificates

- Mortgage/deed statements

- Retirement Pension/Annuity Info
- Social Security Benefits Info

She should be aware of the financial status of the house, knowing what bills are due when, and where and how to pay them. She should have access to all household financial accounts and should know how to save, invest, budget, live within her means, protect her credit rating, and make wise and financially sound decisions.

It's never too early or too late to learn how to financially prepare and protect yourself. Start now. Train your kids how to do the same. It's time to sit down and have the hard conversations. Too many women have been left in a position where they are not able to care for themselves or their families once they are left on their own. Let's change the narrative and be about our business. Prepare now to secure your future.

I used to shy away from the topic of death and preparing for the inevitable. I was too scared to talk about it. But this is such an IMPORTANT conversation. The average cost of a funeral can be over $10k. Too often families are not prepared to cover this expense in such a short amount of time. This can put strain (financial, emotional, etc.) on an already stressful situation.

SETTING UP A LIFE INSURANCE POLICY IS AN ACT OF LOVE!! Don't let fear stop you! The time is NOW to have the hard conversations. Don't wait until it is too late to prepare for the future.

Talk to an expert that can walk you through the process and explain how it all works. What you don't know and don't address CAN hurt you. Knowledge is power.

Make time for you. Don't be so consumed with life that you neglect your own needs. Detox from the world around you. Free your mind and feed your soul. Time spent with God is self-care. Prayer, reading, and meditation on the Word can lead to breakthrough and healing of your most pressing issue. Don't worry (Philippians 4:6-7). He sees and He knows (Psalm 139:1-6). He cares (1 Peter 5:7-9). He'll give you peace (Isaiah 26:3). He'll give you rest (Matthew 11:28). Take time to renew your mind, refresh your spirit, and replenish your heart.

Go from Pain to Purpose. Serving others helps you to take the focus off what you are going through and puts it on meeting the needs of others. When you repurpose your pain, you take your power back because you've gained wisdom, insight, and strength from the pain you have experienced, even if you still feel the effects.

Being a survivor is not just about making it through something. It's about reaching back and helping others to make it out as well. You are proof that it can be done.

Life does not ask for your permission. Learn how to override the way you feel and fall back on what you know to be true. You Are Enough and can make happiness your choice. Healing is a process and takes time. But it won't begin until you move forward in faith and in hope of a better you!

Chapter 12: All I Need Is You

Marriage is a ministry. It is all about service. You are there to meet each other's needs, especially those they cannot meet themselves like love, belonging, and acceptance. In marriage you are both servants. It's a win/win situation as both will have their needs met. By only thinking about yourself and your own needs, you give place to the enemy. You invite him to come in and cause division and disharmony in your home. Meeting needs in marriage means that you die to yourself. What that means is you put your needs aside to make sure that the needs of your spouse are being fulfilled. Meeting your spouse's needs validates their importance to you. It shows that they matter to you. It sends the message that they are heard, seen, and cared for.

A good marriage will meet needs. If not, problems will arise. When you meet the needs of your spouse, you are ensuring and assuring them that they are safe in your relationship with them. Having experienced trauma, their sense of security has been stripped and there is an even greater need to let them know that you are there for them. It will alleviate fear and doubt within the relationship. This can help to reduce the chances of infidelity as they won't look for their needs to be fulfilled outside of your marriage.

Problems in the bedroom, or other areas of the relationship can also lead to infidelity, which can only complicate the issues and worsen the effects of trauma in your life. Remember, the goal of the enemy is to steal, kill, and destroy, which can have a devastating impact on your mental wellbeing.

Infidelity comes with its own set of post-traumatic symptoms. Marriage is a covenant. Your soul, which houses your mind and your emotions, is intertwined with your spouse's soul. A violation of the covenant is more than just physical. It can do damage all the way to the core of your soul, which is your heart.

Can a relationship go back to normal after someone cheats? It depends on the couple. Both have to be willing to rebuild. It takes time, healing, and trust. The work you do to overcome it can actually fix the issues you had in the past and give you a blueprint on how to fix the issues that may come up in the future. The easy thing to do is walk away, but it is not a sign of weakness to stay and work things out. It's not a desirable situation, but if both are willing, and the relationship is worth it to them, they can make it work.

Intimacy starts well before you get to the bedroom. This is where spending time together and getting to know each other comes in. Never think or take for granted that you already know your spouse. People change and grow and enter many different seasons in life. Your job is to get to know the person that they are becoming while trying to understand the person they have been. This will help you to better understand why a person is the way they are, why they react a certain way, and will teach you how to interact with them.

The words you say and the acts of kindness you do for your spouse should be done with the intention of displaying your love and affection for them. Sex is a mind thing, even though we see with our eyes and desire with our hearts. Sex is emotional because our feelings are intertwined. If there is a problem in the bedroom, chances are it didn't start there. The question then becomes "Can I trust you with my heart?"

Trust is about being vulnerable, leaving yourself open to receive from someone else and to give yourself to them. If trust is violated in any way, this can affect the relationship. Trust issues are a type of fear driven by your imagination and based on past experience. It is important not to hold your spouse hostage (or vice versa) to the thoughts that run through your mind. That is simply fear speaking through the pain of the past. Work through your emotions before you unleash them on your spouse. Self-awareness is key in self-control.

Communicate what you need within your relationship and what you expect from your spouse. Be sure your expectations are realistic and doable for the other person. Be open and transparent. Explain to them why you feel the way you do and where these needs you have expressed have come from. Understanding why you feel a certain way will help to break down a communication barrier and lead to empathy where they can see the situation from your point of view. When they have an understanding of why you are the way you are, they will be more careful with your heart and treat you accordingly.

Keep the past in the past and learn to let it go. Don't hold them hostage to the mistakes they made in the past. Forgiveness does not excuse the offender. It protects your heart from bitterness. Seek professional counseling to help you work through difficult issues. An objective point of view may be helpful when you are at an impasse.

Sometimes the answer is just to keep them busy! You know what they say about an idle mind...too much time on their hands can lead to excessive drinking, clouded thinking, and a bad night. GET AHEAD OF IT! Plan something you can do together.

By being proactive in this way, you help to shift their mind back to what is important: Their Emotional Health and Wellbeing and Strengthening Your Relationship. Take time to reconnect as friends and lovers. Date night is a great way to rekindle your love for one another. It helps to reduce stress and tension and opens the line of communication with ease. A night on the town, or on the couch, can be just what the doctor ordered!

I attribute a large part of our healing to the bond my husband and I share over food. Whether it was cooking a meal together or catching a bite at our favorite restaurant, the Dinner Table was a great way to strengthen our bond and encourage the conversations centered around our feelings and emotions. It helped us to reignite our love for one another and empowered us to continue in the fight for our marriage.

Make an effort to walk in love with each other. Forgive constantly and continually. Learn to let go of grudges. Talk through your issues. Listen to what the other is saying. If you have to, ask what they need from you. Sometimes problems in relationships occur because someone has an unmet need that they have not expressed.

Pray that God will make you into the mate that your spouse needs, not just the one they wanted. Marriage is a divine covenant. "A cord of three strands is not easily broken" (Ecclesiastes 4:12). Make God the third strand that binds it all together and gives it strength.

Don't neglect the bedroom. Sex is an important part of marriage. As a spouse, you are the only one in the world that can fulfill this need. Lack of sex causes a buildup of tension and this can lead to bigger problems in your relationship.

Sex is a gift from God. Given not just for procreation, but to enjoy our spouse and strengthen our bond. That is why it is so pleasurable, to encourage us to want to reconnect with one another. Sexual attraction ignites the fire of passion in your relationship.

The Bible says the marriage bed is undefiled, which means that you can let it all hang loose! If you want to be a cheerleader and swing from the chandelier, that's all up to you. Go for it! The connection and intimacy brought on by sex is healthy and healing. Kisses, hugs, and touch are all important methods to connect and rekindle the passion between the two of you, even before you get to the bedroom.

Letting your spouse know that they are loved and desired is a healthy dose of medicine that can aid in reducing the effects of trauma.

When a person feels safe and secure in their relationship with you, it helps to ease anxiety and reduce tension in the relationship.

Patience and understanding are needed on both sides. Be mindful of where your partner is mentally. Never use sex to excuse or avoid toxic behavior. Love does not hurt. Sometimes the two of you will not be on the same page or headspace. If the answer is no, please respect that. Understand that it is not an attack on you. It is just not the time. Come together again once the timing is right.

2 Corinthians 7 explains that the wife's body belongs to her husband and her husband's body belongs to her. It says, "Do not deprive one another- except when you agree for a time, to devote yourselves to prayer. Then come together again; otherwise, Satan may tempt you because of your lack of self-control" (2 Corinthians 7:5, CSB).

Pressuring you to have sex by saying "If you don't do it, someone else will" is another means of emotional manipulation. You should never feel pressured into doing anything you don't want to do. Sex should never be used as a weapon. Never blame yourself for the actions or misdeeds of others. You can only be responsible for your own actions.

Makeup sex does not excuse toxic behavior. In fact, it complicates the issue, adds to the problem, and can make things worse, especially if you are only giving in to pacify the situation (or to avoid further drama). Having sex because you feel pressured to do so is a form of sexual abuse...even if you are married to them. Explosive arguments and physical or verbal aggression reveals a lack of communication skills, respect, and self-control. Problems in your relationship cannot be fixed in the bedroom. Especially if sex is being used as a tool of manipulation.

If you are in an abusive relationship, seek help. Call the National Domestic Violence Hotline: (800)799-7233 or check out their website - https://www.thehotline.org/

He who finds a wife finds a good thing and obtains favor with the Lord. Remember, YOU are a blessing. And don't you forget it.

Forgive them, while holding them accountable. This is for you. Don't excuse behavior. Let go of offense. Don't make others pay for what someone else did to you. All men aren't dogs, just the ones that you have experienced. Don't be a victim. Find the lesson and grow from it. Set a standard. Create boundaries that reflect how you want to be treated. Talk it out. Explain how you feel and why you feel it, giving them a chance to change their behavior.

Some things are within your power to change. Do you complain about your spouse to your family and friends? This can be toxic to your relationship. You may be looking for support and empathy from them, however, this can actually make your problems worse.

It violates trust within the marriage and allows others to step in and voice their opinions about your marriage. It makes your spouse look like they are the only problem and can turn friends and family against them. It can also cause you to focus only on the negative aspects of the relationship, which can lead to serious marital issues.

If you want to stop the drama in your family, stop telling them about what goes on in your relationship. Real love PROTECTS and COVERS. There is a reason that certain things should be kept in the house: To protect the unity and sanctity of that marriage.

So what do you do?

Seek WISE Counsel—Find another married couple that you AGREE ON to help you through relationship issues. Promise to discuss your problems only with them.

Work on your issues TOGETHER. Working to resolve conflict can actually bring you closer to each other. Who better to discuss your marital problems with than the one you are married to!!

Focus on YOURSELF! Remember the saying "Treat people how you want to be treated?" The same goes in marriage. If you focus on your own actions and treat your spouse not in the way they deserve, but how they are SUPPOSED to be treated, this will make them change the way they behave toward you.

"Anxiety weighs down the heart, but a kind word cheers it up" (Proverbs 12:25). Think before you speak. Choose to use words that BUILD. Words that are KIND and that will UPLIFT. Your words are seeds. Speak LIFE to your situation. Speak LIFE to your relationship.

As a wife, you have the power to speak LIFE and HEALING by using your words to validate and affirm them. Speak these words of affirmation to build them up and to reassure their value and position in your life: "You are loved. You are valued. You are desired. I care about your feelings. I respect your opinion. I trust your judgement. You matter to me. I love you. We're in this together. I'm here with you. I'm here for you. We're in this together." Let your words be the seeds and let your actions be the water to make them grow.

Chapter 13: In the Trenches

There are some needs that can only be met by God. As a wife, you are the spiritual covering and first line of defense for your husband. As the one closest to your spouse, your prayers are essential. Pray and ask for guidance on how to be the wife they need you to be specifically for them. Cover your spouse in prayer. Ask God for discernment and the wisdom to handle every situation. Be honest with God and each other about how you feel. Ask for help in understanding and help to deal with the issues at hand.

Stay on guard and be ready for action. Be sensitive to the environment of your home. You are equipped! Watch for danger. Discern the problem and attack it at the root. The best thing you can do as a PTSD Wife is to educate yourself to help you understand what your spouse may be going through and how it can affect your home. You are the watchman on the wall. This will help you to know what to look for.

If your spouse is dealing with grief, give them space to deal with their emotions in their own time and in their own way. Give them your presence. Isolation and loneliness can lead to depression. You don't have to say or do anything. Just be there for them. Give them a break. Help them with everyday errands and chores. This will free them to tend to what is important. Honor the memory of their loved one when they are ready. Reminisce on the good times. Laughter is like medicine (Proverbs 17:22).

Be observant and watch for signs of depression, anxiety, and unhealthy coping methods. Death can trigger intense emotions and lead to toxic behaviors. Encourage professional grief counseling or a support group to work through emotions. Finally, pray for them and pray with them. There is power in unity.

When anxiety attacks, stay calm. Use your words to affirm them and talk them down. Ask them how you can help and let them know that they are safe right now in this moment. Change their focus. Ask them to breathe with you or count backwards from 100. Respect their space. If they don't want to be touched or consoled, or if they don't want to talk, don't force it. Don't take it personal. Your only job is to support them and give them comfort. Make sure YOU are safe and out of harm's way. Preventive care is best in these situations, understanding and avoiding triggers, and seeking professional counseling or treatment. Know the signs and be able to recognize the onset of an episode. Use nature's remedy: A healthy diet, routine exercise, and plenty of rest.

Walking in love does not include treating people the way that they treat you. Love is a mindset that goes well beyond emotions. It is a constant decision to push past how you feel and to do what is right. Even when you are hurting. You cannot control the actions of others, but you can control the way you react. Forgive them and let go of offense. Bitterness can cause emotional and physical side effects. Show compassion and have empathy. Try to see things from their point of view. Above all, extend grace. Give the very thing you would like in return.

In a PTSD relationship, you must learn to guard your heart against feelings of bitterness and resentment. When the smoke clears and they begin to come down from the high of an explosive episode, they will (eventually) realize the hurt and pain they caused in that moment. They may feel guilt for losing control and/or shame for having done it again. Rejection from you can make them spiral deeper into depression, toxic thinking, and toxic behavior. You may have a valid reason to be upset, especially if this is a recurring issue. But you must be careful not to let your anger turn into bitterness or hold a grudge against them. Because at that point, you are not holding them accountable. You are holding them hostage. You are punishing them.

Learn how to process your anger and let it go before it turns into bitterness and resentment. Filter your thoughts. Accept what is true. Reject what is not. Don't act on your emotions. Take time to cool down. You can't take back the things you say or do in anger. Some damage cannot be reversed. Redirect your energy. Change your focus to what calms you and brings you peace. Address issues head on so they don't continue to fester. Timing is everything. Wait until you both are in a position to receive what the other is saying. Practice empathy. Learn to see things from their perspective and show compassion. Let it go! Bitterness is a root that can lead to emotional and physical sickness.

Forgiving them does not excuse toxic or abusive behavior. Your safety and wellbeing are priority. Seek professional counseling for help with anger management. Forgiveness is a process. It is a constant decision to keep moving forward despite the challenges that will come. Being able to move past offense is a sign of your strength and your character.

What if they DON'T WANT to get help? You can't help someone

who doesn't realize or accept that they need help. They may not think they need it, or simply just don't want it. Maybe they are not ready to move forward with change yet. They may not be ready to put in the work to make changes.

As a PTSD Wife, it is NOT your job to FIX them! The decision must come from them when they are ready. Don't take this rejection personal. Instead, talk it out. Communication is key. Use "I" statements. Tell them how YOU are feeling without placing blame on them. Refrain from "You" statements (You always...You never...). Say It with Love: What you say is just as important as HOW you say it. Remember, timing is everything! Make sure you talk to them when they are in the right headspace to receive what you are saying. Create a Crisis Kit and have it ready for emergencies:

- Emergency Contacts

- Important Documents

- List of Medications

- List of Triggers/Coping Mechanisms

- List of Effective Calming Techniques

If you call 911, be sure to let them know what mental condition your loved one is dealing with.

Put together a list of resources that you can turn to for help. Your local suicide prevention line or website, a trusted friend or family members that can help you when things spiral out of control. My father-in-law is so good with talking Straight Talk to my husband. He is someone whom he respects, and he knows that he would never tell him anything to lead him down the wrong path. Having someone like this in your life is such a blessing.

Seek professional help. A trained counselor, pastor, coach, or therapist to help you work through your issues. It is important that as you do the work to uncover your issues and trauma, that you don't get stuck and relive the pain. A trained professional will help you to work through the pain and find your way out.

Keep a list of emergency rooms and/or crisis centers in your area. It is best to be ready in case of emergency so you don't have to scramble to get the information in the heat of the moment when you may not be thinking straight.

For any spouse, you must keep important documents in a secure place so you can know where to find them. Birth certificates, Social Security cards, health insurance cards, ID cards, military DD214, wills, power of attorney, and other court documents. This can save you time and help you avoid being frustrated in those already stressful moments.

Be observant. Learn your spouse's triggers and try to head them off. Triggers are connected to painful memories or emotional wounds that have not healed. Triggers are also connected to anxiety, which is rooted in FEAR (False Evidence Appearing Real). You must be proactive. Know what triggers your spouse and understand the effect it has on them. Help them to avoid the trigger, but don't try to protect them from it. They must learn for themselves how to navigate their way through tough situations. Show compassion and empathy but hold them accountable for their actions. Reaffirm your love and validate your feelings for them. Reassure them of your commitment. The best way to do this is to take up time with them. "An idle mind is the devil's workshop." Although that is not an actual scripture, it is great advice. You have to keep them busy to keep their mind from wandering and subject to attack. Quality time will help you escape your "real world" and gives you a way to focus on what is really important, your unity. Find something fun that you like to do together and can keep you engaged in conversation, laughter, and love.

Some things are not meant for us to be rescued from. We have to go through it. Look for the lesson, increase your faith, and build your strength. Learn how to grow from your adversity. Tough times don't last, but tough people do. The strength of your marriage cannot be measured by what you did not have to go through, but by what you overcome together.

The secret to longevity in marriage is found in Colossians 3:12-15: "Clothe yourselves with Compassion, Kindness, Humility, Gentleness, and Patience. Bear with each other and forgive one another if any of you has a grievance. Forgive as the Lord forgave you. Above all, put on LOVE, which binds them all together in perfect unity. And let the PEACE of Christ rule your hearts. And be thankful."

Chapter 14: After the Storm

In this day and age, I know it is hard to have any hope. We can get frustrated with the way things are going, thinking things will never change. We must be patient in trouble and be consistent in prayer. Our faith requires that we hang in there and keep trusting and believing that things will work out in the end. We have to believe it before we can see it. You must keep praying for your spouse, your family, and yourself.

Continue to envision the life you want and keep working toward it. It will be worth the wait.

Have patience. Patience will build your endurance. It will help develop your character and perfect you. God is patient with us, and we must be patient with each other.

God is getting you ready for the things He has promised you. It may not look like it now, and you may not understand it, but the time will come when you will be able to look back and understand why you had to come through this storm the way you did.

Give it time. God doesn't let us have some things because we are not ready for them. Perhaps, there is more work we need to do. If God hands us everything at the exact moment that we want it, we may misuse or abuse it. It may even kill us. We have some growing to do so He can perfect us for our promise. Jesus is our example of how we are to walk in love. He had compassion on all those that were sick and suffering. We are all a work in process.

Be patient in trouble. Keep praying. It takes time to restore what has been broken. Your strength will be tested. This will give you the opportunity to be patient, forgiving and compassionate with one another.

Frustration is connected to what you are expecting. Waiting will test your faith thinking that God is not going to do it for you. You've done everything in your own power, but have you tried giving it to God to let Him work it in His power?

The key is to change your focus. If you only focus on what is wrong in your marriage, you will never appreciate what is right. Learn to have an attitude of gratitude. You will find what you seek. If you are only seeking to find the negative, that is what will stand out the most. But if you look for the good things, remember the best times, and think back on why you fell in love in the first place, you will get a new outlook on things. That person is still in there. Maybe they just need you to bring it out of them.

Change does not happen overnight. It is a process. The process is the road you must take to get you to your goal. In this case, your goal is inner peace, self-love, and personal strength. It involves sacrifice. The process will cost you. No pain, no gain. But here's a secret...You need the process in order to fully develop you for the prize. There are no shortcuts. No easy button. You had to go through the hard times you've experienced because they were developing you to get to where the Lord wants to take you.

The process is the part of the journey that develops you. It sharpens your skills and challenges the way you think. The pain and hard times you have faced and are facing now are designed to make you spiritually, mentally, and emotionally stronger. When you finally get to your goal you will be able to look back and see all the things you went through and all you had to overcome. You will find that you are still standing. A survivor.

The next time you face a challenge in life or in marriage, remember all that you have gone through and have faith that the lessons learned from your past experience will empower you to overcome and move on to the next goal. One day, you are going to look back and see just how far you have come. After all you have been through, you are still standing. It did not break you. It only made you stronger. Make up in your mind that you will not return to the way things used to be.

Do not let fear, doubt, and uncertainty get the best of you. Too many times we have allowed the fear of the unknown, and the fear of what we think we know to stop us from accomplishing the things we want in life. You can't be so scared to fail that you never even try in the first place!

It's time to stop letting fear rule over your life! The best way to overcome fear is to face it! You cannot overcome what you do not face. Consider the steps you need to take to accomplish the mission and execute the plan. Your mindset is key. You have to see yourself as victorious from the start! Make a decision to finish, no matter what, and press toward your goal.

Don't give up! You've come too far to stop now!

Some things are within your power to control. Take time to work on yourself. Don't lose yourself in the process of trying to help your spouse. It is important to maintain your own identity and continue to pursue your interests and goals. Take classes, start a business, write a book. What is that thing that you have been longing to do, but never did? You will find that by doing what brings you joy, you will be healing yourself along the way.

Use your past as fuel to go from pain to purpose. Serving others changes your focus from what you are going through to meeting the needs of others. When you repurpose your pain, you take your life back. It's all about you changing the narrative.

Being a survivor is not about proving how blessed you are. It is about reaching back and helping someone else to come out of the place that you have already come out of. Don't be afraid to tell your story. Someone needs to hear it. You are proof that it can be done.

Be the change you want to see in your relationship. Don't wait for them to make the first move. Choose the way of Love. Love is more than just a word...it is a TOOL!! You can use it to build and strengthen. You can use it to protect and cover. If you withhold it, you are still using it...but to tear down and destroy. Walking in Love is not always the easiest thing to do, but it IS the most powerful. Love IS the power to change your situation. While you can't control what someone says or does, you do have the power to control what you say or do in return. It is not a sign of weakness to forgive and to look past the offense or the offender. The real battle is in your mind. Fight to maintain your peace, both inward and outward.

Pain is a part of the process. It is inevitable. It is important to allow yourself time to sit with it. Process your emotions. Accept the lesson. Seek out the blessing. Don't get stuck. A new day is coming. The clouds will roll away. And you will be better having gone through it.

Don't let what you see get in the way of what you know. It may not look like it now, but a new day is coming. You're going to see what you've been praying for. You have power within to speak your change into existence (Romans 4:17). To move obstacles out of your way (Mark 11:23). To breathe life back into your situation (Ezekiel 37:1-10). Keep pushing, keep praying, and keep speaking those things that be not as though they were until they are.

Until then, I pray this blessing over you:

I pray for peace and unity among your family. I pray that your relationships be restored and that the hurt of your past is healed. I pray for a change of heart for the one considering walking away.

I pray for unity over your house. I speak peace in your dwelling, and peace in your heart that you be reconciled to one another. Let there be a refreshing wind of change in your home.

I pray God will bring back the love, affection, and romance between you, even better than it was in the beginning. That you will see each other with new eyes, with a renewed desire and your heart of stone be made flesh.

I pray God molds you to be who you need to be for your spouse and your spouse for you.

I declare that the enemy will NOT have your marriage.

Let there may be healing in your home. Depression, Anxiety, and Fear be gone! May God send the help and resources you need to be delivered.

Thank you, Lord that you hear our prayers and are quick to hasten over your word. Thank you for the miracles you will perform in our hearts, in our home, and in our marriage.

You get the glory and the honor, God.

"Now unto him who is able to do exceedingly and abundantly above all that you can ask or think..."

Be Encouraged. Be Empowered. And Be Blessed.

www.ingramcontent.com/pod-product-compliance
Lightning Source LLC
Chambersburg PA
CBHW051432090426
42737CB00014B/2940